How to Start & Manage a Restaurant Business

A Practical Way to Start Your Own Business

by Jerre G. Lewis and Leslie D. Renn

How to Start & Manage A Restaurant Business

Lewis & Renn Associates, Inc.

Business & Professional Publishing

10315 Harmony Drive
Interlochen, Michigan 49643
(231) 275-7287

Leslie D. Renn
President

Jerre G. Lewis
Secretary-Treasurer

ISBN # 978-1-57916-160-6
Library of Congress Catalog Card Number
99-094197

TABLE OF CONTENTS

Chapter 1

Introduction

Selecting the right Restaurant business opportunity requires careful, thorough evaluations of yourself. Owning your own business is as much a part of the American dream as owning a home, and for you, this urge represents one of life's most exciting challenges. This book is for those men and women who someday may go into business for themselves and for those who are already in business for themselves but wish to strengthen their entrepreneurial and managerial skills.

Entrepreneurs come in all shapes and sizes, personalities, and lifestyles. They are usually highly motivated, hard-working individuals who receive satisfaction from taking risks. Your business should interest you, not just be an income generator. Analyze your personal style. Do you like working with people? Are you a self starter, goal oriented, persistent, a risk taker, willing to work hard and long hours?

If you have been honest in evaluating yourself, you will now select the right type of business. Before you can determine which of the multitude of businesses is right for you to start, you must evaluate the businesses you want to start by asking these questions. Is the business area growing? How does the economy affect it? Who dominates its market? Once you have considered a business that satisfies your needs and interest you must prepare a formal business plan by following the outline given in this book.

Small businesses constitute a dynamic and critical sector of the U.S. economy. Every year in the United States more than 600,000 new businesses are launched by independent men and women eager to make their own decisions, express their own ideas, and be their own bosses. But running your own business is not as easy as it may seem. There can be problems with the inventory, or getting the right goods delivered on time. Yet, managing one's own business can be a personally and financially rewarding experience for an individual strong enough to meet the test. A person with stamina, maturity, and creativity, one who is willing to make sacrifices, may find making a go of a struggling enterprise an exhilarating challenge with many compensations.

Small business owners are a dedicated group of people who work hard and whose hours on the job usually exceed the nine-to-five routine. The owner's commitment is the key to many successful small businesses; an entrepreneur is able to communicate ideas, lead, plan, be patient, and work well with people.

Managing a business requires more than the possession of technical knowledge. Because most small businesses are started by technical people, such as engineers and salesmen, their managerial acumen is often less developed than their technical skills. The need to plan for management is common to every type of and size of business, and there are certain steps that must be taken. Although some of them are very elementary — such as applying for a city business permit — the most important are often complex and difficult and require the advice of specialists: accountants, attorneys, insurance brokers, and/or bankers. For almost any business though, the first step will be to translate the entrepreneur's basic idea into a concrete plan for action.

To gauge your level of entrepreneurial spirit, the following quiz was created. Please answer each question honestly and then total the columns.

ENTREPRENEURIAL QUIZ

	YES	NO	SOMETIMES
1. I am a self-starter. Nobody has to tell me how to get going.	_____	_____	__________
2. I am capable of getting along with just about everybody.	_____	_____	__________
3. I have no trouble getting people to follow my lead.	_____	_____	__________
4. I like to be in charge of things and see them through.	_____	_____	__________
5. I always plan ahead before beginning a project. I am usually the one who gets everyone organized.	_____	_____	__________
6. I have a lot of stamina. I can keep going as long as necessary.	_____	_____	__________
7. I have no trouble making decisions and can make up my mind in a hurry.	_____	_____	__________
8. I say exactly what I mean. People can trust me.	_____	_____	__________
9. Once I make my mind up to do something, nothing can stop me.	_____	_____	__________
10. I am in excellent health and have a lot of energy.	_____	_____	__________

	YES	NO	SOMETIMES
11. I have experience or technical knowledge in the business I intend to start.	____	____	________
12. I feel comfortable taking risks if it is something I really believe in.	____	____	________
13. I have good communication skills.	____	____	________
14. I am flexible in my dealings with people and situations.	____	____	________
15. I consider myself creative and resourceful.	____	____	________
16. I can analyze a situation and take steps to correct problems.	____	____	________
17. I think I am capable of maintaining a good working relationship with employees.	____	____	________
18. I am not a dictator. I am willing to listen to employees, customers and suppliers.	____	____	________
19. I am not rigid in my policies. I am willing to adjust to meet the needs of employees, customers, and suppliers.	____	____	________
20. More than anything else, I want to run my own business.	____	____	________

Total of Column #1 ____________

Total of Column #2 ____________

Total of Column #3 ____________

If the total of Column #1 is the highest, then you will probably be very successful in running your own business.

If the total of Column #2 is the highest, you may find that running a business is more than you can handle.

If the total of Column #3 is the highest, you should consider taking on a partner who is strong in your weak areas.

NOTE: This quiz was adapted from the Small Business Administration publication *Checklist for Going Into Business.*

Notes

Chapter 2

Planning the Business

The Dream of self-employment can be fulfilled. You don't need to finance the opening of an elaborate office or facility to start your own one-person corporation either. You can start your own Restaurant business.

Anyone preparing to run an Restaurant business needs to learn a great deal to assure the best possible chance for success.

GETTING STARTED

The following is a list of what you need to accomplish to insure that your Restaurant endeavor will head in the right direction.

1. Define your educational background and work experience.
2. Survey all the basic types of Restaurant businesses.
3. Define what products or services your Restaurant business will be marketing.
4. Define who will be using your products/services.
5. Define why they will be purchasing your products/services.
6. List all competitors in your Restaurant marketing area.

ZONING REGISTRATIONS

Restaurant businesses are subject to many laws and regulations enforced by state, county, township governmental units. Most jurisdictions now have codes, a zoning board, and an appeal board which regulate businesses. Areas often are zoned residential, commercial or industrial.

You must become familiar with these regulations. If you are doing business in violation of these regulations, you could be issued a cease and desist order or fined.

Certain kinds of goods cannot be produced in the home, though these restrictions vary somewhat from state-to-state. Most states outlaw home production of fireworks, drugs, poisons, explosives, sanitary/medical products and some toys.

Many localities have registration requirements for new businesses. You will need to obtain a work certificate or license from the state.

TAX REQUIREMENTS

<u>Application for Employer Identification Number</u>, Form SS-4. This registers you with the Internal Revenue Service as a business. If you have employees, you should ask for Circular E along with your ID number. Circular E explains federal income and social security tax withholding requirements.

<u>Employer's Annual Unemployment Tax Return</u>, Form 940. This is only if you have employees. It's used to report and pay the Federal Unemployment Compensation Tax.

<u>Employee's Withholding Allowance Certificate</u>, W-4. Every employee must complete the W-4 so the proper amount of income tax can be withheld from the

employee's pay. If the employee claims more than 15 allowances or a complete withholding exemption while having a salary of more than $200 a week, a copy of the W-4 must go to the IRS.

Employer's Wage and Tax Statement, W-2. Used to report to the IRS the total taxes withheld and total compensation paid to each employee per year.

Reconciliation/Transmittal of Income and Tax Statements, W-3. Used to total all information from the W-2. Sent to the Social Security Administration.

The IRS puts on monthly workshops on understanding and using these forms. Call your local IRS office for further information.

States also have various tax form requirements including: an unemployment tax form, a certificate of registration application, a sales and use tax return, an employer's quarterly contribution and payroll report, an income tax withholding registration form, an income tax withholding form, and others. Some forms apply only to employers who have employees. Your local IRS office and state Office of Taxation can provide you with listings of forms you will need to start your business. The following table outlines Federal tax form requirements.

Every small business begins with an idea — a product to be manufactured or sold, a service to be performed.

Whatever the business or its degree of complexity, the owner needs a business plan in order to transform a vision into a working operation.

This business plan should describe in writing and in figures the proposed Restaurant business and its products, services, or manufacturing processes. It should also include an analysis of the market, a marketing strategy, an organizational plan, and measurable financial objectives.

WHAT SHOULD A BUSINESS PLAN COVER?

It should be a thorough and objective analysis of both personal abilities and business requirements for a particular product or service. It should define strategies for such functions as marketing and production, organization and legal aspects, accounting and finance. A business plan should answer such questions as:

What do I want and what am I capable of doing?
What are the most workable ways of achieving my goals?
What can I expect in the future?

There is no single best way to begin. What follows is simply a guide and can be changed to suit individual needs.

1. Define Long-term goals.
2. State short-term.
3. Set marketing strategies to meet goals and objectives.
4. Analyze available resources.
5. Assemble financial data.
6. Review plan.

Please refer to Figure 2.1 for a complete business plan outline.

The business operator with a realistic plan has the best chance for success.

Figure 2.1

BUSINESS PLAN FOR SMALL BUSINESSES

I. Type of Business

II. Location

III. Target Market

IV. Planning Process

V. Organizational Structure

VI. Staffing Procedures

VII. Market Strategy

IX. Financial Planning

X. Budgeted Balance Sheet

XI. Budgeted Income Statement

XII. Budgeted Cash Flow Statement

XIII. Break-Even Chart

Notes

Chapter 3

Marketing Strategies for an Restaurant Business

As a potential Restaurant business owner, it is important to learn all you can about marketing. You will need to know how to identify your market and how to market your product or service.

As a business person who looks for a profit from the sale of goods, you recognize that without people who want to buy, there is no demand for the things you want to sell. Thus, it is important that, in addition to knowing about the functions of marketing, you also study the activities that will influence the consumer. When you satisfy the specific needs and wants of the customer, then he or she may be willing to pay you a price that will include a profit for you — and to make a profit is one of the reasons you have become an Restaurant business owner. Although there are many activities connected with marketing, most of them can be classified in these categories: buy, finance, transport, standardize, store, insure, advertise and sell.

Target Market Analysis

Before you can create a successful marketing campaign, it's necessary to determine your target market (toward whom to direct your energies). The whole concept of target marketing can seem very scary at first. On the surface, targeting appears to be limiting the scope of the pool of potential customers. Many people fear that by defining a market, they will lose business. They are concerned that they will choose the wrong market. Or that other practitioners will take just anybody and therefore some of their business.

You must keep in mind that the purpose of defining your target market is to make your life easier and increase the productivity of your promotional endeavors. Many opportunities exist in this world and it's impossible to pursue them all or be everything to everyone. You need to know where to focus your energy and money when it comes to promotion and advertising.

The two most common means of market analysis are demographics and psychographics, which describe a person in terms of objective data and personality attributes.

Demographics are statistics such as:

- age
- gender
- income level
- geographic location
- occupation
- education level

Psychographics are lifestyle factors including:

- special interest activities
- philosophical beliefs
- social factors
- cultural involvements

The more you know about your potential customers, the easier it is to develop an appropriate position statement and design an effective marketing campaign. The actual number of target markets you have depends mainly upon the size of your practice and the scope of your knowledge.

Your Target Market Profile

In order to clarify your target market(s) you need to delineate the demographic and psychographic factors and then identify the characteristics your customers have in common.

Describe your current customers and those who are most likely your future customers:

What is the age range and average age of your customers?

What is the percentage of males?

What is the percentage of females?

What is the average educational level of your customers?

Where do your customers live?

What are the occupations of your customers?

Where do your customers work?

What is the average annual income level of your customers?

Of what special interest groups are your customers members?

What is the primary reason your customers use your services?

Defining Your Target Market(s)

Write a descriptive statement for each of your target markets (refer to your "Target Market Profile"). Include a brief overview of the services you are providing to that group and a detailed analysis of the characteristics of the specific clientele.

Target Market 1:

Target Market 2:

Target Market 3:

Restaurant Business Marketing

The foundation for creating a thriving customer base.

A. Overview

This section is about clarifying your beliefs and attitudes toward your profession and determining the image you wish to portray.

1. Describe the "character" that you want for your business.
   Depict the image you want to convey:

2. State your philosophy in regard to your business:

3. Describe your philosophy regarding your practice in business:

B. Customer Profile

This is a descriptive analysis of your current and potential customers — who they are, what their interests are, and where you can find them. Include each of your target markets.

1. Target Market 1:

2. Target Market 2:

3. Target Market 3:

C. Competition's Marketing Assessment

The first phase in planning your promotional campaign is appraising the competition. List each of your major competitors and describe the marketing strategies they utilize. Be certain to include where and how often they advertise.

1. Major Competitor 1:

2. Major Competitor 2:

3. Major Competitor 3:

4. Major Competitor 4:

5. Major Competitor 5:

6. Major Competitor 6:

Restaurant Marketing Planning

Outline for Marketing:

I. Produce/Service Concept
   A. Name of produce or service
   B. Descriptive characteristics of product or service
   C. Unit sales
   D. Analysis of market trends

II. Number of Customers in Market Area:
   A. Profile of customers
   B. Average customer expenditure
   C. Total market

III. Your Market Potential:
   A. Total market divided by competition
   B. Total market multiplied by percent who will buy your product

IV. Needs of Customers:
   A. Identification
   B. Pleasure
   C. Social approval
   D. Personal interest
   E. Price

V. Direct Marketing Sources:
   A. Trade magazines
   B. Trade associates
   C. Small Business Administration (SBA)
   D. Government publications
   E. Yellow Pages
   F. Marketing directories

VI. Customer Profile:
   A. Geographical
   B. Gender
   C. Age range
   D. Income brackets
   E. Occupation
   F. Educational level

Chapter 4

Promoting the Restaurant Business

When a new business is opened, the owner must be prepared to publicize the business or its chance for success will be slim. Only a few businesses — such as those with a prime location, nationally known name, or a built-in clientele — can succeed without advertising to promote market awareness and stimulate sales.

The first purpose — promoting customer awareness — applies as much to established businesses as to newcomers.

In the Restaurant business, you will find it easier to retain old customers than to win new ones. When old customers move away from your area, or when their buying needs change, you need new customers to maintain your sales volume. If you expect your business to gain, you will need additional new customers. New customers are those who move into your area or who have grown into your line of products because now they can afford them or they need them. We see advertising and we hear advertising all around us, and yet that is only a part of it. Through advertising, you call the attention of customers to your products.

As a small business owner, you may advertise your business through your location. People pass by and are attracted to your operation because of what you are selling. To get a better idea of what advertising is, consider some of the following functions of advertising:

1. ***To inform:*** Letting customers know what you have for sale through brochures, leaflets, newspapers, radio, TV, and etc.

2. ***Persuade:*** Persuasion is the art of leading individuals to do what you want them to do. There are sales personnel who have persuasive sales presentations, but persuasion in advertising is nonpersonal. The appeal is made through the printed or spoken words or a picture. The influence of an ad on readers occurs as purchasers choose what they want among different products, and different wants. To gain the actions you want — a sale — you must persuade a customer to examine personally what you have for sale.

3. ***Reminder:*** Advertising performs it's third function when it reminds those who have been persuaded to buy once that the same product will bring satisfaction. The ad will also remind a customer of the characteristics of a product purchased some time ago, and where he or she bought it. Because customers change their loyalty to a place of business, their taste for products, and often their trading area patronage, advertising is necessary to draw new customers and to hold old customers. To generate results from advertising that will be profitable to your business, you will have to produce answers to the what, where and how of advertising.

What to Advertise

The nature of your business will partially answer the question "Shall I advertise goods or services?" What are the outstanding features of your business? Is it unique in any way? Does it have strong points? Do you have something to offer that the competition is not able to duplicate? Answers to these questions will give you a start in deciding what to advertise.

Where to Advertise

Of course, you will want to advertise within your marketing area, however there are a few guidelines to remember:

A. Who are your customers?
B. What is their income range?
C. Why do they buy?
D. How do they buy? Do they pay Cash? Charge?
E. What is the radius of your market area?

How to Advertise:

In determining how to advertise, you will have to consider your dollar allocation for advertising and the media suitable to your particular kind of business. However, it is important to have a balance between the presentation of the product or service being advertised and the application of three basic principles.

1. Gain the attention of the audience.
2. Establish a need.
3. Tell where that need may be filled.

See Figure A for an outline of the different advertising media and Figure B for budget on media goals.

Figure A

Advertising Media

Media	Market Coverage	Type of Audience
Daily Newspaper	Single community or entire metro area; zoned editions sometimes available	General
Weekly Newspaper	Single community	Residents
Telephone Directory	Geographical area or occupational field served by the directory	Active shoppers for goods or services
Direct mail audience	Controlled by the advertiser	Controlled
Radio audience	Definable market area	Selected
Television audience	Definable market area	Various
Outdoor	Entire metro area	General auto drivers
Magazine	Entire metro area or magazine region	Selected audience

Figure A

Promotion and Advertising Plan — Restaurant Business

In designing your promotional plan, it's wise to use a variety of media. You must have specific goals, time lines and budgets for each marketing application

Media	Goal	Timeline	Budget

Notes

Chapter 5

Financial Planning for an Restaurant Business

Financial planning is the process of analyzing and monitoring the financial performance of your business so you can assess your current position and anticipate future problem areas. The daily, monthly, seasonal, and yearly operation of your business requires attention to the figures that tell you about the firm's financial health.

Maintaining good financial records is a necessary part of doing business.

The increasing number of governmental regulations alone makes it virtually impossible to avoid keeping detailed records. Just as important is to keep them for yourself. The success of your business depends on them. An efficient system of record keeping can help you to:

- make management decisions
- compete in the marketplace
- monitor performance
- keep track of expenses
- eliminate unprofitable merchandise
- protect your assets
- prepare your financial statements

Financial skills should include understanding of the balance sheet, the profit-and-loss statement, cash flow projection, break-even analysis, and source and application of funds. In many businesses, the husband and wife run the business; it is especially important that both of them understand financial management. Most small business owners are not accountants, but they must understand the tool of financial management if they are going to be able to measure the return on their investment. Although good records are essential to good financial planning, they alone are not enough because their full use requires interpretation and analysis. The owner/manager's financial decisions concerning return on invested funds, approaches to banks, securing greater supplier credit, raising additional equity capital and so forth, can be more successful if he takes the time to develop understanding and use of the balance sheet and profit-and-loss statement.

Balance Sheet:

The balance sheet, Figure I, shows the financial condition of a business at the end of business on a specific day. It is called a balance sheet because the total assets balance with, or are equal to, total liabilities plus owner's capital balance. Current assets are those that the owner does not anticipate holding for long. This category includes cash, finished goods in inventory, and accounts receivable. Fixed assets are long-term assets, including plant and equipment. A third possible category is the intangible asset of goodwill. Liabilities are debts owed by the business, including both accounts payable, which are usually short-term, and notes payable, which are usually long-term debts such as mortgage payments. The difference between the value of the assets and the value of the liabilities is the capital. This category includes funds invested by the owner plus accumulated profits, less withdrawals.

The Income Statement:

This statement, Figure II, is also known as a profit-and loss (P&L) statement. It shows how a business has performed over a certain period of time. An income statement specifies sales, costs of sales, gross profit, expenses and net income or loss from operations.

Figure I

Financial Forecast

Opening Balance Sheet - Date

ASSETS		
Current Assets		
Cash and bank accounts		$
Accounts receivable		$
Inventory		$
Other current assets		$ ________
TOTAL CURRENT ASSETS	(A)	$ ________
Fixed Assets		
Property owned		$
Furniture and equipment		$
Business automobile		$
Leasehold improvements		$
Other fixed assets		$ ________
TOTAL FIXED ASSETS	(B)	$ ________
TOTAL ASSETS	(A+B = X)	$ ________
LIABILITIES		
Current Liabilities (due within the next 12 months)		
Bank loans		$
Other loans		$
Accounts payable		$
Other current liabilities		$ ________
TOTAL CURRENT LIABILITIES	(C)	$ ________
Long-term Liabilities		
Mortgages		$
Long-term loans		$
Other long-term liabilities		$ ________
TOTAL LONG-TERM LIABILITIES	(D)	$ ________
TOTAL LIABILITIES	(C+D = Y)	$ ________
NET WORTH	(X-Y = Z)	$ ________
TOTAL NET WORTH AND LIABILITIES	(Y+Z)	$ ________

Figure II

Business Income and Expense Forecast for the Next 12 Months

One year estimate ending ______________________________, 19 _____

Projected Number of Clients

For your services	________
For your products	________
TOTAL NUMBER OF CLIENTS	________

Projected Income

Sessions	$ ________
Product sales	$ ________
Other	$ ________
TOTAL INCOME	$ ________

Projected Expenses

Start-up costs	$ ________
Monthly expenses (x 12)	$ ________
Annual expenses	$ ________
TOTAL EXPENSES	$ ________
TOTAL OPERATING PROFIT (OR LOSS)	$ ________
CAPITAL REQUIRED FOR THE NEXT 12 MONTHS	$ ________

Start-Up Costs Worksheet	
Item	**Estimated Expense**
Open checking account	$
Telephone installation	$
Equipment	$
First & last month's rent, security deposit, etc.	$
Supplies	$
Business cards, stationery, etc.	$
Advertising and promotion package	$
Decorating and remodeling	$
Furniture and fixtures	$
Legal and professional fees	$
Insurance	$
Utility deposits	$
Beginning inventory	$
Installation of fixtures and equipment	$
Licenses and permits	$
Other	$
TOTAL	$

Fixed Annual Expense Worksheet	
Item	**Estimated Expense**
Property insurance	$
Business auto insurance	$
Licenses and permits	$
Liability insurance	$
Disability insurance	$
Professional society membership	$
Fees (legal, accounting, etc.)	$
Taxes	$
Other	$
TOTAL	$

Monthly Business Expense Worksheet		
Expense	**Estimated Monthly Cost**	**X 12**
Rent	$	$
Utilities	$	$
Telephone	$	$
Bank fees	$	$
Supplies	$	$
Stationery and business cards	$	$
Networking club dues	$	$
Education (seminars, books professional journals, etc.)	$	$
Business car (Payments, gas, repairs, etc)	$	$
Advertising and promotion	$	$
Postage	$	$
Entertainment	$	$
Repair, cleaning and maintenance	$	$
Travel	$	$
Business loan payments	$	$
Salary/Draw	$	$
Staff salaries	$	$
Miscellaneous	$	$
Taxes	$	$
Professional fees	$	$
Decorations	$	$
Furniture and fixtures	$	$
Equipment	$	$
Inventory	$	$
Other	$	$
TOTAL MONTHLY	$	$
TOTAL YEARLY		$

Cash Flow Forecast						
	January Estimate	**January Actual**	**February Estimate**	**February Actual**	**March Estimate**	**March Actual**
Beginning cash						
Plus monthly income from: Fees						
Sales						
Loans						
Other						
TOTAL CASH AND INCOME						
Expenses:						
Rent						
Utilities						
Telephone						
Bank fees						
Supplies						
Stationery and business cards						
Insurance						
Dues						
Education						
Auto						
Advertising and promotion						
Postage						
Entertainment						

Cash Flow Forecast (Continued)						
	January Estimate	**January Actual**	**February Estimate**	**February Actual**	**March Extimate**	**March Actual**
Repair and maintenance						
Travel						
Business loan payments						
Licenses and permits						
Salary/Draw						
Staff salaries						
Taxes						
Professional fees						
Decorations						
Furniture and fixtures						
Equipment						
Inventory						
Other Expenses						
TOTAL EXPENSES						
ENDING CASH (+/-)						

Notes

Chapter 6

Restaurant Business Planning

Introduction

Our increasingly service oriented economy offers a widening spectrum of opportunities for customized and personalized small business growth. Though untrained entrepreneurs have traditionally had a high rate of failure, small businesses can be profitable. Success in a small Restaurant business is not an accident. It requires both skills in a service or product area and acquisition of management and attitudinal competencies.

The purpose of this publication is to help you take stock of your interests, aptitudes and skills. Many people have good business ideas but not everyone has what it takes to succeed. If you are convinced that a profitable Restaurant business is attainable, this publication will provide step-by-step guidance in development of the basic written business plan.

Information Gathering

A helpful tool for use in determining if you are ready to take the risks of an Restaurant business operation is the SMA publication entitled *Going Into Business* (MP-12).

It will help you focus on the basic steps in information gathering and business planning.

Careful planning is required to research legal and tax issues, proper space utilization and to establish time management discipline. Inadequate or careless attention to development of a detailed business plan can be costly for you and your family in terms of lost time, wasted talent and disappearing dollars.

The Entrepreneurial Personality

A variety of experts have documented research that indicates that successful small business entrepreneurs have some common characteristics. How do you measure up? On this checklist, write a "Y" if you believe the statement describes you; a "N" if it doesn't; and a "U" if you can't decide:

_____ I have a strong desire to be my own boss.

_____ Win lose or draw, I want to be master of my own financial destiny.

_____ I have significant specialized business ability based on both my education and my experience.

_____ I have an ability to conceptualize the whole of a business; not just its individual parts, but how they relate to each other.

_____ I develop an inherent sense of what is "right" for a business and have the courage to pursue it.

_____ One or both of my parents were entrepreneurs; calculate risk-taking runs in the family.

_____ My life is characterized by a willingness and capacity to preserver.

_____ I possess a high level of energy, sustainable over long hours to make the business successful.

While not every successful Restaurant business owner starts with a "Y" answer to all of these questions, three or four "N"s and "U"s should be sufficient reason for you to stop and give a second thought to going it alone. Many proprietors who sense entrepreneurial deficiencies seek extra training a support their limitations with help from a skilled team of business advisors such as accountants, bankers and attorneys.

Selecting a Business

A logical first step for the undecided is to list potential areas of personal background, special training, education and job experience, and special interests that could be developed into a business. Review the following list of activities which have proven marketable for others. On a scale of "0" (no interest or strength) to "10" (maximum interest or strength) indicate the potential for you and a total score for each activity.

Time Management

For both the novice and the experienced business person planning a small Restaurant enterprise, an early concern requiring self-evaluation is time management.

It is very difficult for some people to make and keep work schedules even in a disciplined office setting. As your own boss the problem can be much greater. To determine how much time you can devote to your business, begin by drafting a weekly task timetable listing all current and potential responsibilities and the blocks of time required for each. When and how can business responsibilities be added without undue physical or mental stress on you or your family? Potential conflicts must be faced and resolved at the outset and as they occur, otherwise your business can become a nightmare. During the first year of operation, continue to chart, post and checkoff tasks on a daily, weekly and monthly basis.

Distractions and excuses for procrastination abound. It is important to keep both a planning and operating log. These tools will help avoid oversights and provide vital information when memory fails.

To improve the quality of work time, consider installation of a telephone line for the business and attaching an answering machine to take messages when you do not wish to be distracted or are away from your business. A business line has the added advantage of allowing you to have a business listing in the phone book and if you wish to buy it, an ad in the classified directory.

Is an Restaurant Business Site Allowable?

Now you will want to investigate potential legal and community problems associated with operating the business. You should gather, read and digest specialized information concerning federal, state, county and municipal laws and regulations concerning Restaurant business operations.

Check first! Get the facts in writing. Keep a topical file for future reference. Some facts and forms will be needed for your business plan. There may be limitations enforced that can make your planned business impossible or require expensive modifications to your property.

Items to be investigated, recorded and studied are:

TO DO	DONE	
______	______	county or city zoning code restrictions
______	______	necessary permits and licenses for operation
______	______	state and local laws and codes regarding zoning
______	______	deed or lease restrictions such as covenants and restrictive conditions of purchase

_____	_____	parking and customer access; deliveries
_____	_____	sanitation, traffic and noise codes
_____	_____	signs and advertising
_____	_____	state and federal code requirements for space, ventilation, heat and light
_____	_____	limitations on the number and type of workers. If not, check with the local Chamber of Commerce office
_____	_____	reservations that neighbors may have about a business next to or near them

Here are some ways to collect your information. Call or visit the zoning office at county headquarters or city hall. In some localities the city or county Office of Economic Development has print materials available to pinpoint key "code" items affecting a business.

Even in rural areas, the era of unlimited free enterprise is over. Although the decision makers may be in the state capital or in a distant regional office of a federal agency, check before investing in inventory, equipment or marketing programs. If in doubt, call the state office of Industrial Development or the nearest SBA district office. In some states the county agent or home demonstration agent will have helpful information concerning rural or farm business development.

Is the Business Site Insurable?

In addition to community investigations, contact your insurance company or agent. It is almost certain that significant changes will be required in your coverage and limits when you start a business. When you have written a good description of your business, call your agent for help in insuring you properly against new hazards resulting from your business operations such as:

- Fire, theft and casualty damage to inventories and equipment
- business interruption coverage
- fidelity bonds for employees
- liability for customers, vendors and others visiting the business
- workmen's compensation
- group health and life insurance
- product liability coverage if you make or sell a product; workmanship liability for services
- business use of vehicle coverage

Overall Restaurant Site Evaluation

After you have gathered as much information as seems practical you may wish to evaluate several different locations. Here's a handy checklist. Using the "0" to "10" scale, grade these vital factors:

Factors to Consider

Factor	**Grades 0-10**
1. Customer convenience	_____
2. Availability of merchandise or raw materials	_____
3. Nearby competition	_____
4. Transportation availability and rates	_____
5. Quality and quantity of employees available	_____
6. Availability of parking facilities	_____

7. Adequacy of utilities (sewer, water, power, gas) _____

8. Traffic flow _____

9. Tax burden _____

10. Quality of police and fire services _____

11. Environmental factors _____

12. Physical suitability for future expansion _____

13. Provision for future expansion _____

14. Vendor delivery access _____

15. Personal convenience _____

16. Cost of operation _____

17. Other factors including how big you get without moving _____

TOTALS _____

Writing the Business Plan

Now that your research and plan development is nearing completion, it is time to move into action. If you are still in favor of going ahead, it is time to take several specific steps. The key one is to organize your dream scheme into a business plan.

What is it?

- As a business plan it is written by the Restaurant business owner with outside help as needed
- It is accurate and concise as a result of careful study
- It explains how the business will function in the marketplace
- It clearly depicts its operational characteristics
- It details how it will be financed
- It outlines how it will be managed
- It is the management and financial "blueprint" for start-up and profitable operation
- It serves as a prospectus for potential investors and lenders

Why create it?

- The process of putting the business plan together, including the thought that you put in before writing it, forces you to take an objective, critical, unemotional look at your entire business proposal
- The finished written plan is an operational tool which, when properly used, will help you manage your business and work toward its success
- The completed business plan is a means for communicating your ideas to others and provides the basis for financing your business

Who should write it?

- The Restaurant owner to the extend possible
- Seek assistance in weak areas, such as:
  - — accounting
  - — insurance
  - — capital requirements
  - — operational forecasting
  - — tax and legal requirements

When should a business plan be used?

- To make crucial start-up decisions
- To reassure lenders or backers
- To measure operations progress
- To test planning assumptions
- As a basis for adjusting forecasts
- To anticipate ongoing capital and cash requirements
- As the benchmark for good operations management

Proposed Outline for Restaurant Business Plan

This outline is suggested for a small proprietorship or family business. Shape it to fit *your* unique needs. For more complex manufacturing or franchise operations see the Resource section for other options.

Part I - Business Organization

Cover page:

A. Business name:
Street address:
Mailing address:
Telephone number:
Owner(s) name(s):

Inside pages:

B. Business form:
(proprietorship, partnership, corporation)

If incorporated (state incorporation)

Include copies of key subsidiary documents in an appendix.

Remember even partnerships require written agreements of terms and conditions to avoid later conflicts and to establish legal entities and equities. Corporations require charters, articles of incorporation and bylaws.

Part II - Business Purpose and Function

In this section, write an accurate yet, concise description of the business. Describe the business you plan to start in narrative form.

What is the principal activity? Be specific. Give product or service description(s):

- retail sales?
- manufacturing?
- service?
- other?

How will it be started?

- a new start up
- the expansion of an existing business
- purchase of a going business
- a franchise operation
- actual or projected start up date

Why will it succeed? Promote your idea!

- how and why this business will be successful
- what is unique about your business
- what is its market "niche"

What is your experience in this business? If you have a current resume of your career, include it in an appendix and reference it here. Otherwise write a narrative here and include a resume in the finished product. If you lack specific experience, detail how you plan to gain it, such as training, apprenticeship or working with partners who have experience.

The Marketing Plan

The marketing plan is the core of your business rationale. To develop a consistent sales growth an Restaurant business person much become knowledgeable about the market. To demonstrate your understanding, this section of the Restaurant business plan should seek to concisely answer several basic questions:

Who is your market?

- Describe the profile of your typical customer
  Age?
  Male, female, both?
  How many in family?
  Annual family income?
  Location?
  Buying patterns?
  Reason to buy from you?

Other?

- Biographically describe your trading area (i.e., county, state, national)
- Economically describe your trading area: (single family, average earnings, number of children)

How large is the market?

- Total units or dollars?
- Growing ____ Steadily ____ Decreasing ____
- If growing, annual growth rate. ______________________

Who is your competition?

No small business operates in a vacuum. Get to know and respect the competition. Target your marketing plans. Identify direct competitors (both in terms of geography and product lines), and those who are similar or marginally comparative. Begin by listing names, addresses and products or service. Detail briefly but concisely the following information concerning each of your competitors:

- Who are the nearest ones?
- How are their businesses similar or competitive to yours?
- Do you have a unique "niche"? Describe it.
- How will your service or product be better or more saleable than your competitors?

- Are their businesses growing? Stable? Declining? Why?
- What can be learned from observing their operations or talking to their present or former clients?
- Will you have competitive advantages or disadvantages? Be honest!

What percent of the market will you penetrate?

1. estimate the market in total units or dollars
2. estimate your planned volume
3. amount your volume will add to total market
4. subtract 3 from 2

Item 4 represents the amount of your planned volume that must be taken away from the competition.

What pricing and sales terms are you planning?

The primary consideration in pricing a product or service is the value that it represents to the customer. If, on the previous checklist of features, your product is truly ahead of the field, you can command a premium price. On the other hand, if it is a "me too" product, you may have to "buy" a share of the market to get your foothold and then try to move price up later. This is always risky and difficult. One rule will always hold: ultimately, the market will set the price. If your selling price does not exceed your costs and expenses by the margin necessary to keep your business healthy, you will fail. Know your competitors pricing policies. Send a friend to comparison shop. Is there discounting? Special sales? Price leaders? Make some "blind" phone calls. Detail your pricing policy.

What is your sales plan?

Describe how you will sell, distribute or service what you sell. Be specific. Below are outlined some common practices:

Direct Sales - by telephone or in person. The tremendous growth of individual sales representatives who sell by party bookings, door to door, and through distribution of call back promotional campaigns suggests that careful research is required to be profitable.

Mail Order - Specialized markets for leisure time or unique products have grown as more two income families find less time to shop. Be aware of recent mail order legislation and regulation.

Franchising -

a. You may decide to either buy into someone else's franchise as a franchisee, or

b. Create your own franchise operation that sells rights to specific territories or product lines to others. Each will require further legal, financial and marketing research.

Management Plan

Who will do what?

Be sure to include four basic sets of information:

1. State a personal history of principals and related work, hobby or volunteer experience (include formal resumes in Appendix)

2. List and describe specific duties and responsibilities of each

3. List benefits and other forms of compensation for each

4. Identify other professional resources available to the business: Example: Accountant, lawyer, insurance broker, banker. Describe relationship of each to business: Example "Accountant available on part-time hourly basis, as needed, initial agreement calls for services not to exceed x hours per month at $xx.xx per hour."

To make this section graphically clear, start with a simple organizational chart that lists specific tasks and shows, *who* (type of person is more important than an individual name other than for principals) will do *what* indicate by arrows, work flow and lines of responsibility and/or communications. Consider the following examples:

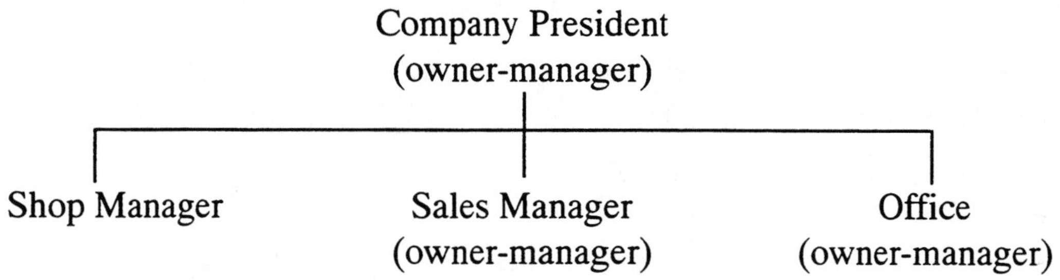

or like this?

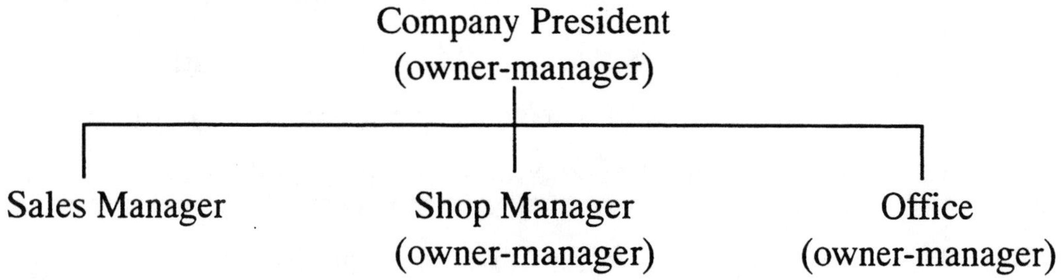

As the service business grows, its organization chart could look like this:

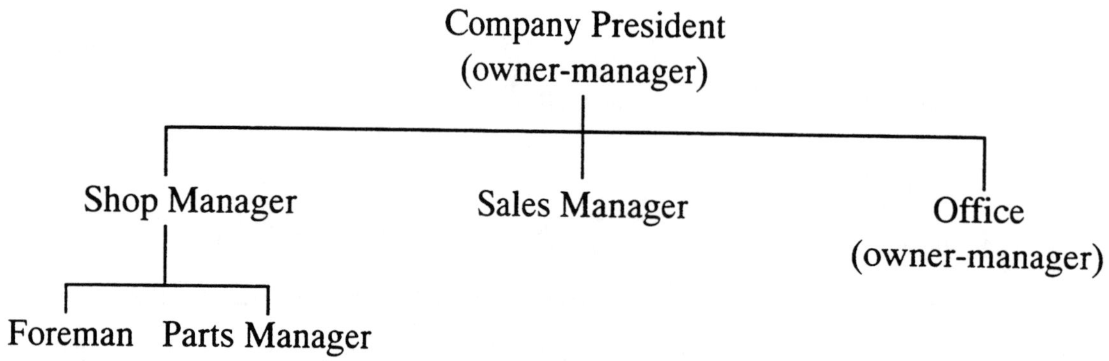

The Financial Plan

Clearly the most critical section of your business plan document is the financial plan. In formulating this part of the planning document, you will establish vital schedules that will guide the financial health of your business through the troubled waters of the first year and beyond.

Before going into the details of building the financial plan, it is important to realize that some basic knowledge of accounting is essential to the productive management of your business. If you are like most business owners, you probably have a deep and abiding interest in the product or services that you sell or intend to sell. You like to do what you do, and it is even more fulfilling that you are making money doing it. There is nothing wrong with that. Your conviction that what you are doing or making is worthwhile is vitally important to success. Nonetheless, the income of a coach who takes the greatest pride in producing a winning team will largely depend on someone keeping score of the wins and losses.

The business owner is no different. Your product or service may improve the condition of mankind for generations to come, but, unless you have access to an unlimited bankroll, you will fail if you don't make a profit. If you don't know what's going on in your business, you are not in a very good position to assure its profitability.

Most Restaurant businesses will use the "cash" method of accounting with a system of record keeping that may be little more than a carefully annotated checkbook in which is recorded all receipts and all expenditures, backed up by a few forms of original entry (invoices, receipts, cash tickets). For a Sole Partnership, the business form assumed by this Management Aid, the very minimum of recorded information is that required to accurately complete the Federal Internal Revenue Service Form 1040, Schedule C. Other business types (partnerships, joint ventures, corporations) have similar requirements but use different tax forms.

If your business is, or will be, larger than just a small supplement to family income, you will need something more sophisticated. Stationery stores can provide you with several packaged small business account systems complete with simple journals and ledgers and detailed instructions in understandable language.

Should you feel that your accounting knowledge is so rudimentary that you will need professional assistance to establish your accounting system, the classified section of your telephone directory can lead you to a number of small business services that offer a complete range of accounting services. You can buy as much as you need, from a simple "pegboard" system all the way to computerized accounting, tax return service and monthly profitability consultation. Rates are reasonable for the services rendered and an investigative consultation will usually be free. Look under the heading, "Business Consultants," and make some calls.

Let's start by looking at the makeup of the financial plan for the business.

The Financial plan includes the following:

1. Financial Planning Assumptions - these are short statements of the conditions under which you plan to operate.

- Market health
- Date of start-up
- Sales build-up ($)
- Gross profit margin
- Equipment, furniture and fixtures required
- Payroll and other key expenses that will impact the financial plan

2. Operations Plan - Profit and Loss Projection - this is prepared for the first year's Budget. Appendix A-11.

3. Source of Funds Schedule - this shows the source(s) of your funds to capitalize the business and how they will be distributed among your fixed assets and working capital.

4. Pro Forma Balance Sheet - "Pro forma" refers to the fact that the balance sheet is before the fact, not actual. This form displays Assets, Liabilities and Equity of the business. This will indicate how much Investment will be required by the business and how much of it will be used as Working Capital in its operation.

5. Cash Flow Projection - this will forecast the flow of cash into and out of your business through the year. It helps you plan for staged purchasing, high volume months and slow periods.

Creating the Profit and Loss Projection.

Appendix A-11. Create a wide sheet of analysis paper with a three inch wide column at the extreme left and thirteen narrow columns across the page. Write at the top of the first page the planned name of your business. On the second line of the heading, write "Profit and Loss Projection." On the third line, write "First Year."

Then, note the headings on Appendix A-11 and copy them onto your 12-column sheet, copy the headings from the similar area on Exhibit A. Then follow the example set by Appendix A-11 and list all of the other components of your income, cost and expense structure. You may add or delete specific loans of expense to suit your business plan. Guard against consolidating too many types of expenses under one account lest you lose control of the components. At the same time, don't try to break down expenses so discretely that accounting becomes a nuisance instead of a management tool. Once again, Exhibit A provides ample detail for most businesses.

Now, in the small column just to the left of the first monthly column, you will want to note which of the items in the left-hand column are to be estimated on a monthly (M) or yearly (Y) basis. Items such as Sales, Cost of Sales and Variable expenses will be estimated monthly based on planned volume and seasonal or other estimated fluctuations. Fixed Expenses can usually be estimated on a yearly basis and divided by twelve to arrive at even monthly values. The "M" and "Y" designations will be used later to distinguish between variable and fixed expense.

Depreciation allowances for Fixed Assets such as production equipment, office furniture and machines, vehicles, etc. will be calculated from the Source of Funds Schedule.

Appendix A-11 describes line by line how the values on the Profit and Loss Projection are developed. Use this as your guide.

Source of Funds Schedule

To create this schedule, you will need to create a list of all the Assets that you intend to use in your business, how much investment each will require and the source of funds to capitalize them. A sample of such a list is shown below:

Asset	Cost	Source of Funds
Cash	$2,500	Personal savings
Accounts Receivable	3,000	From profits
Inventory	2,000	Vendor credit
Pickup truck	5,000	Currently owned
Packaging machine	10,000	Installment purchase
Office desk and chair	300	Currently owned
Calculator	75	Personal cash
Electric typewriter*	500	Personal savings

* A note about office equipment, test use or rent two or more brands that appear to meet your needs and select the one with which you feel most comfortable. Don't be afraid to ask others who have had to make this decision for advice. Compatibility of your system with those of potential typesetting services or printers should be of high considerations. If you are not quite sure, consider renting or leasing the equipment until you are. Service contracts on such complex electronic gear are usually a good insurance policy.

Before you leave your Source of Funds Schedule, indicate the number of months (years x 12) of useful life for depreciable fixed assets. (An example, the pickup truck, the packaging machine and the furniture and office equipment would be depreciable.) Generally, any individual item of equipment, furniture, fixtures, vehicles, etc., costing over $100 should be depreciated. For more information on allowances for depreciation, you can get free publications and assistance from your local Internal Revenue Service office. Divided the cost of each fixed asset item by the number or months over which it will be depreciated. You will need this data to enter as monthly depreciation on your Profit and Loss Projection. All of the data on the Source of Funds Schedule will be needed to create the Balance Sheet.

Creating the Pro Forma Balance Sheet

Appendix A-13. This is the Balance Sheet Form. There are a number of variations of this form and you may find it prudent to ask your banker for the form that the bank uses for small business. It will make it easier for them to evaluate the health of your business. Use this to get started and transfer the data to your preferred form later. Accompanying Appendix A-12 which describes line by line how to develop the Balance Sheet.

Even though you may plan to stage the purchase of some assets through the year, for the purpose of this pro forma Balance Sheet, assume that all assets will be provided at the start-up.

Cash Flow Projection

An important subsidiary schedule to your financial plan is a monthly Cash Flow Projection. Prudent business management practice is to keep no more cash in the business than is needed to operate it and to protect it from catastrophe. In most small businesses, the problem is rarely one of having too much cash. A Cash Flow Projection is made to advise management of the amount of cash that is going to be absorbed by the operation of the business and compares it against the amount that will be available.

SBA has created an excellent form for this purpose and it is shown as Appendix B. Your projection should be prepared on 13-column analysis paper to allow for a twelve-month projection. Appendix B represents a line by line description and explanation of the components of the Cash Flow Projection which provides a step-by-step method of preparation.

Resources

U.S. Small Business Administration
Office of Business Development

Business Development Publication
MP15

Restaurant Business Associations for the Entrepreneur

Educational Foundation of the National Restaurant Assoc. (EFNRA)
205 S. Wacker Dr., No. 1400
Chicago, IL 60606
Daniel A. Gescheidle, Pres.
PH: (312) 715-1010 TF: (800) 765-2122
Founded: 1971 Nonmembership

National Assoc. of Restaurant Managers (NARM)
Address unknown since 1994
Founded: 1986 Members: 350

National Restaurant Assoc. (NRA)
1200 17th St. NW
Washington, DC 20036
William P. Fisher, Exec. VP
Founded: 1919 Members: 20,000

Notes

Chapter 7

Managing The Business

Delegating work, responsibility, and authority is difficult in a small business because it means letting others make decisions which involved spending the owner/manager's money. At a minimum, he should delegate enough authority to get the work done, to allow assistants to take initiative, and to keep the operation moving in his absence. Coaching those who carry responsibility and authority in self-improvement is essential and emphasis in allowing competent assistants to perform in their own style rather than insisting that things be done exactly as the owner/manager would personally do them is important. "Let others take care of the details" is the meaning of delegating work and responsibility. In theory, the same principles for getting work done through other people apply whether you have 25 employees and one top assistant or 150 to 200 employees and several keymen yet, putting the principles into practice is often difficult.

Delegation is perhaps the hardest job owner/managers have to learn. Some never do. They insist on handling many details and work themselves into early graves. Others pay lip service to the idea but actually run a one-man shop. They give their assistants many responsibilities but little or no authority. Authority is the fuel that makes the machine go when you delegate word and responsibility. If an owner/manager is to run a successful company, he must delegate authority properly. How much authority is proper depends on your situation. At a minimum, you should delegate enough authority: (1) to get the work done, (2) to allow keymen to take initiative, (3) to keep things going in your absence.

The person who fills a key management spot in the organization must either be a manager or be capable of becoming one. A manager's chief job is to plan, direct, and coordinate the work of others. He should possess the three "I's" — Initiative, Interest, and Imagination. The manager of a department must have enough self-drive to start and keep things moving. Personality traits must be considered. A keyman should be strong-willed enough to overcome opposition when necessary.

When you manage through others, it is essential that you keep control. You do it by holding a subordinate responsible for his actions and checking the results of those actions. In controlling your assistants, try to strike a balance. You should not get into a keyman's operations so closely that you are "in his hair" nor should you be so far removed that you lose control of things.

You need feedback to keep yourself informed. Reports provide a way to get the right kind of feedback at the right time. This can be daily, weekly, or monthly depending on how soon you need the information. Each department head can report his progress, or lack of it, in the unit of production that is appropriate for his activity; for example, items packed in the shipping room, sales per territory, hours of work per employee.

For the owner/manager, delegation does not end with good control. It involves coaching as well, because management ability is not required automatically. You have to teach it. Just as important, you have to keep your managers informed just as you would be if you were doing their jobs.

Part of your job is to see that they get the facts they need for making their decisions. You should be certain that you convey your thinking when you coach your assistants. Sometimes words can be inconsistent with thoughts. Ask questions to make sure that the listener understands your meaning. In other words, delegation can only be effective when you have good communications.

Sometimes an owner/manager finds himself involved in many operational details even though he does everything that is necessary for delegation of responsibility. In spite of defining authority, delegation, keeping control, and coaching, he is still burdened with detailed work. Usually, he had failed to do one vital thing. He has refused to stand back and let the wheels turn.

If the owner/manager is to make delegation work, he must allow his subordinates freedom to do things their way. He and the company are in trouble if he tries to measure his assistants by whether they do a particular task exactly as he would do it. They should be judged by their results — not their methods. No two persons react exactly the same in every situation. Be prepared to see some action taken differently from the way in which you would do it even though your policies are well defined. Of course, if an assistant strays too far from policy, you need to bring him back in line. You cannot afford second-guessing.

You should also keep in mind that when an owner/manager second-guesses his assistants, he risks destroying their self-confidence. If the assistant does not run his department to your satisfaction and if his shortcomings cannot be overcome, then replace him. But when results prove his effectiveness, it is good practice to avoid picking at each move he makes.

Notes

Chapter 8

Business Resource Information

Books

Steps To: Small Business Start-up,
by Linda Pinson and Jerry Jinnett (Kaplan Publishing, 2006).

Blue's Clues for Success: The 8 Secrets Behind a Phenomenal Business,
by Diane Tracy (Dearborn, 2001).

Entrepreneur Magazine's Start Your Own Business, 3rd. ed.,
by Rieva Lesonsky (Entrepreneur Press, 2004).

MBA in a Day: What You Would Learn at the Top-Tier Business Schools,
by Steven Stralser (New York: John Wiley & Sons, 2004).

Own Your Own Corporation: Why the Rich Own Their Own Companies and Everyone Else Works for them,
by Garrett Sutton, Robert T. Kiyosaki, and Ann Blackman (Warner Books, 2001).

Portratis of Success: 9 Keys to Sustaining Value in Any Business,
by James Olan Hutcheson (Dearborn, 2002).

Small Time Operator: How to Start Your Own Business, Keep Your Books, Pay Your Taxes, and Stay Out of Trouble, (Small Time Operator, 27th Edition)
by Bernard B. Kamoroff, (Bell Springs Publishing, 2005).

Successful Business Planning in 30 Days: A Step-by-Step Guide for Writing a Business Plan and Starting Your Own Business,
by Peter J. Patsula (Patsul Media, 2000).

Straight Talk About Starting and Growing Your Business,
by Sanjyot P. Dunung (McGraw Hill, 2006).

Associations and Organizations

U.S. Department of Commerce
14th Street and Constitution Avenue NW
Room 5055
Washington, DC 20210
Phone: 202-482-5061
Web site: *rvwm.mbda.gov*

U.S. Department of Labor
200 Constitution Avenue NW
Washington, DC 20210
Web site: *www.dol.gov*

Federal Trade Commission
600 Pennsylvania Avenue NW
Washington, DC 20580
General information: 202-326-2222
Anti-trust and competition issues: 202-326-3300
Web site: *www.ftc.gov*

U.S. Small Business Administration (SBA)
403 3rd Street SW
Washington, DC 20416
Phone: 202-205-7701
Web site: *www.sba.gov*

SBA Regional Offices

- Region 1, Boston: 617-565-8415
- Region 2, New York: 212-264-1450
- Region 3, King of Prussia, PA: 215-962-3700
- Region 4, Atlanta: 404-347-995
- Region 5, Chicago: 310-353-5000
- Region 6, Ft. Worth, TX: 817-885-6581
- Region 7, Kansas City, MO: 816-374-6380
- Region 8, Denver: 303-844-0500
- Region 9, San Francisco: 415-744-2118
- Region 10, Seattle: 206-553-7310

Internal Revenue Service
Washington, DC 20224
Phone: 800429-1040
Web site: *www.irs.ustres.gov*

The IRS has an expansive Web site where you can find a great deal of tax help and a state-by-state guide for locating state tax information. There are also numerous tax publications (all numbered) including:

- Tax Guide for Small Business, Publication #3
- Self-Employment Tax, Publication #533
- Business Expenses, Publication #535

For tax forms go to *www.irs.ustres.gov/forms*

International Franchise Association
1350 New York Avenue NW
Suite 900
Washington, DC 20005-4709
Phone: 202-628-8000

American Association of Franchises and Dealers
P.O. Box 81887
San Diego, CA 92138-1887
Phone: 800-733-9858
Web site: *www.aafd.org*

Associations and Organizations

National Association of Women Business Owners
1411 K Street NW
Suite 1300
Washington, DC 20005
Phone: 202-347-8686
Fax: 202-347-4130
Information service line: 800-556-2926
Web site: *www.nawbo.org*

The National Association for the Self-Employed
1023 15 Street NW
Suite 1200
Washington, DC 20005-2600
Phone: 202-466-2100
Web site: *www.nase.com*
The NASE works to help the self-employed make their businesses successful and provides numerous benefits and services. It was formed over twenty years ago by small business owners.

Occupational Safety and Health Administration (OSHA)
200 Constitution Avenue NW
Washington, DC 20210
Web site: *www.osha-slc.gov*

Institute For Occupational Safety and Health
Phone: 800-35-NIOSH or 513-533-8328
Web site: *www.cdc.gov/niosh*

Dun & Bradstreet
Austin, Texas 78731
Phone: 800-234-3867
Web site: *www.dnb.com*
For over 160 years, D&B has been providing companies with information and assistance in making key business decisions.

American Entrepreneurs for Economic Growth
1655 North Fort Myer Drive
Suite 850
Arlington, VA 22209
Phone: 703-524-3743
Web site: *www.aeeg.org*

National Association of Home-Based Businesses
10451 Mill Run Circle
Suite 400
Owings Mills, MD 21117
Phone: 410-363-3698
Web site: *www.usahomebusiness.com*

U.S. Census Bureau
Washington DC 20233
Phone: 301-457-4608
Web site: *www.census.gov*

U.S. Patent and Trademark Office
General Information Services Division
Crystal Plaza 3, Room 2CO2
Washington, DC 20231
Phone: 800-786-9199 or 703-308-4357
Web site: *www.uspto.gov*

U.S. Securities & Exchange Commission
450 Fifth Street NW
Washington, DC 20549
Office of Investor Education and Assistance: 202-942-7040
Web site: *www.sec.gov*

Associations and Organizations

**American Association of
Home Based Businesses**
Fax: 301-963-7042
P.O. Box 10023
Rockville, MD 20849
Website: *www.aahbb.org*

American Small Businesses Association
800-942-2722
8773 IL Route 75E
Rock City, IL 61070

Home Business Institute
561-865-0865
P.O. Box 480215
Delray Beach, FL 33448
Website: *www.hbiweb.com*

Marketing Research Association
860-257-4008
1344 Silas Deane Highway, Suite 306,
Rocky Hill, CT 06067
Website: *www.mra-net.org*

**National Association of the
Self-Employed (NASE)**
800-252-NASE (800-232-6273)
P.O. Box 612067
DFW Airport
Dallas, TX 75261-2067
Website: *www.nase.org*

Magazines

Entrepreneur Magazine, Business Start-Ups Magazine, and **Entrepreneur's Home Office**
Entrepreneur Media, Inc.
2392 Morse Avenue
Irvine, CA 92614
Phone: 714-261-2325
Web site: *www.entrepreneurmag.com*

Forbes
60 Fifth Avenue
New York, NY 10011
Phone: 212-620-2200
Web site: *www.forbes.com*

Inc. Magazine
38 Commercial Wharf
Boston, MA 02110
Phone: 617-248-8000 or 800-2340999
Web site: *www.inc.com*

My Business Magazine
Hammock Publishing, Inc.
3322 West End Avenue
Suite 700
Nashville, TN 37203
Phone: 615-385-9745

Consumer Goods Manufacturer
Edgell Communications
10 West Hanover Avenue
Suite 107
Randolph, NJ 07869

Minority Business Entrepreneur
3528 Torrance Boulevard
Suite 101
Torrance, CA 90503
Phone: 310-540-9398
Web site: *www.mbemag.com*

Workforce ACC Communications
245 Fischer Avenue
Suite B-2
Costa Mesa, CA 92626
Phone: 714-751-4106
Web site: *www.workforceonline.com*

Websites

www.allbusiness.com
A comprehensive site with resources for small and medium sized businesses.

www.bizweb.com
A guide to some 47,000 companies.

www.bplan.com
Numerous sample business plans for various industries.

www.bspage.com
The Business Start page includes a short course on starting a business, tips, and reviews of top business books.

www.business.gov
The U.S. Business Advisor is a one-stop shop for working with the many government agencies that impact upon business.

www.businessfinance. com
A major online source for finding potential investors.

www.businessnation.com
Business news, a library, discussions, opportunities, and resources.

www.businesstown.com
Information and articles from starting to selling your business.

www.catalogconsultancy.com
Information and guidance for catalog and direct mail businesses.

www.chamber-of-commerce.com
Links to local chamber of commerce Web sites, and e-mail addresses.

www.financenet.com
Sponsored by the US Chief Financial Officers Council, FinanceNet has a wealth of information and resources available specializing in public financial management.

www.globalbizdirectory.com
Massive director of retail, agricultural, mining and numerous other business-related organizations and associations. Includes a state-by-state and international listing database.

www.gomez.com
Gomez offers business new and detailed report cards and consumer responses on e-commerce Web sites in various sectors.

www.homebusiness.com
Detailed information and business solutions for the home base business.

www.hoovers.com
Provides detailed business and company information, industry report links, professional help, business news, and more.

www.ideacafe.com
A good place for news, tips, expert advice ideas, and schmoozing with other small business owners.

www.inc.com
A wealth of articles and advice about starting and growing your business from the folks at Inc. Magazine.

www.marketingsource.com/associations
Find any association in any industry at this valuable resource site.

www.morebusiness.com
Articles, tips, sample business and marketing plans, legal forms contracts, a newsletter, and more offered for entrepreneurs.

www.nasbic.org
The National Association of Small Business Investment Companies promotes growth in the business sector through numerous programs.

Library Resources

Almanac of Business and Industrial Financial Ratios
(Prentice-Hall). Provides ratios and industry norms in actual dollar figures derived from IRS data. Each industry includes performance indicators such as total assets, cost of operations, wages, and profit margins.

American Wholesaler and Distributor Directory
(Gale Research). Provides listings of wholesalers and distributors sorted by product category and state.

Catalog of Catalogs
(Woodbine House). Contains descriptions and contact information for more than 14,000 catalogs, indexed by subject and company name.

Directory of Manufacturers' Sales Agencies
(Manufacturing Agents National Association). Lists manufacturers' sales agencies alphabetically and by state. Also has information on how to select a sales agent.

Encyclopedia of Associations
(Gale Research). Guise to national and international associations; contains contact information and descriptions; indexed by name, key word, and geographic area.

Financial Studies of the Small Business
(Financial Research Associates). Organized by industry; contains financial ratios and indicators for small and microbusinesses.

Lifestyle Market Analyst
(Standard Rate & Data Service). Reference book containing demographic and psychographic statistics for metropolitan statistical areas in the United States.

Small business Profiles
(Gale Research). Contains sources of information related to starting specific types of small businesses. Typical entries include start-up information, trade associations and publications, statistics, and supply sources.

Thomas Food Industry Register.
Directory of food manufacturers and suppliers to the food industry.

Thomas Register of Manufacturing.
Directory of most manufacturing firms; includes company profile and contact information.

The Small Business Administration

The U.S. Small Business Administration was established in 1953 to provide financial, technical, and management assistance to entrepreneurs. Statistics show that most small business failures are due to poor management. For this reason, the SBA places special emphasis on business management training that covers such topics as planning, finance, organization, and marketing. Often, training is held in cooperation with educational institutions, chambers of commerce, and trade associations. Prebusiness workshops are held on a regular basis for prospective business owners. Other training programs are conducted that focus on special needs such as rural development and international trade. One-on-one counseling is provided through the Service Corps of Retired Executives (SCORE) and Small Business Development Centers (SBDC). The SBA strives to match the needs of a specific business with the expertise available.

To access the SBA: Online http://www.sba.gov
SBA Answer Desk 800-827-5722

SCORE is a volunteer program that helps small business owners solve their operating problems through free one-on-one counseling and through a well-developed system of low-cost workshops and training sessions. To located a SCORE counseling center in your area or to consult online, access the following site: http://www.score.org

SBDCs are generally located or headquartered in academic institutions and provide individual counseling and practical training for prospective and current business owners. To locate a center near you, log on to http://www.sba.gov/sbdc.

Appendix A

A Concise Guide To Starting Your Own Business

Guide Overview

A concise overview of the complete guide to starting and operating a successful business.

The following topics are presented:

- Business Plan for Small Businesses.
- Getting Started
- Deciding Where To Start The Business
- Business Patronage Statistics
- Site Location
- Site Selection Criteria — Some General Questions.
- Choosing The Proper Method of Organization
- What Is A Corporation?
- Estimating Start-up Costs
- Preparing An Income Statement
- Preparing A Balance Sheet
- Marketing The Business
- Marketing Planning — An Outline for Marketing
- Advertising Media
- Management and Getting The Work Done
- Sample Organization Chart
- Summary of the Business Plan
- Guide Summary
- Reference Materials

Business Plan for Small Businesses

I. Type of Business
II. Location
III. Target Market
IV. Planning Process
V. Organizational Structure
VI. Staffing Procedures
VII. Control
VIII. Market Strategy
IX. Financial Planning
X. Budgeted Balance Sheet
XI. Budgeted Income Statement
XII. Budgeted Cash Flow Statement
XIII. Break-even Chart

Page A-4

Getting Started

Following is a list of what you need to accomplish to insure that your business endeavor will head in the right direction.

1. Define your educational background and work experience
2. Survey all basic types of businesses.
3. Define what type of business matches your experience and educational background.
4. Choose only the business that you would like to own and operate.
5. Define what products or services your business will be marketing.
6. Define who will be using your products/services.
7. Define why they will be purchasing your products/services.
8. List all competitors in your marketing area.

Deciding Where to Start the Business

Will your business fulfill a need in the area you plan to bring your business to? This section provides you with some important information you need to examine before taking your ideas any further:

1. Decide where you want to live.
2. Choose several areas that would match your priorities.
3. Use the list that follows as a guide to see if your location will match the estimated population needed to support your business. The numbers which follow the type of business indicate the typical number of inhabitants per year.

Business Patronage Statistics

Food Stores
- Grocery Stores 1,534
- Meat and Fish (Sea Food) Markets ... 17,876
- Candy, Nut, and Confectionery Stores .. 31,409
- Retail Bakeries 12,563
- Dairy Products Stores ... 41,587

Eating and Drinking
- Restaurant, Lunch Rooms . 1,583
- Cafeterias 19,341
- Refreshment Places 3,622
- Drinking Places 2,414

General Merchandise
- Variety Stores 10,373
- General Merchandise 9,837

Apparel/Accessories Stores
- Women's Ready-To-Wear Stores 7,102
- Women's Accessory and Specialty Stores 25,824
- Men's and Boy's Clothing and Furnishings 11,832
- Family Clothing 16,890
- Shoe Stores 9,350

Furniture, Home Furnishings, and Equipment Stores
- Furniture Stores 7,210
- Floor Covering 29,543
- Drapery, Curtains, and Upholstery Stores 62,585
- House, Appliances 12,485
- Radios and TV's 20,346
- Record Shops 112,144
- Musical Instruments 46,332

Building Materials, Hardware, and Farm Equipment Dealers
- Lumber and other Building Materials Dealers 8,124
- Paint, Glass, and Wallpaper Stores 22,454
- Hardware Stores 10,206
- Farm Equipment Dealers . 14,793

Automotive Dealers
- Motor Vehicle Dealers, New and Used Cars 6,000
- Motor Vehicle Dealers, Used Cars only 17,160
- Tire, battery, and Accessory Dealers 8,800

Boat Dealers 61,500

Household Trailer Dealers . 44,746

Gasoline Service Stations ... 1,395

Miscellaneous
- Antique and Secondhand Stores 17,170
- Book and Stationery Stores 28,580
- Drugstores 4,268
- Florists 13,531
- Fuel Oil Dealers 25,000
- Garden Supply Stores ... 65,000
- Gift, Novelty Shops 26,000
- Hobby, Toy, and Game Shops 61,000
- Jewelry Stores 13,400
- Optical Goods Stores 62,800
- Sporting Goods Store 27,000

From *Starting and Managing a Small Business of Your Own, 1973;* Small Business Administration, Washington, DC

Page A-6

Site Location

1. Define your number of inhabitants per store.
2. Locate several sites/locations that will match your inhabitants per stores.
3. Define population and its growth potential.
4. Define local ordinances and zoning regulations that you will need in order to start your type of business.
5. Define your trading area and all competitors in your trading area.
6. Define parking need, for your kind of business.
7. Define special needs, etc., lighting, heating, ventilation.
8. Define rental cost of site/location.
9. Define why customers will come to your site/location.
10. Define the future of your site/location as to population growth.
11. Define your space needs and match with site/location selection.
12. Define the image of your business and make sure it matches your site/location.

Site Selection Criteria — Some General Questions

- Is the site centrally located to reach my market?
- What is the transportation availability and what are the rates?
- What provisions for future expansion can I make:
- What is the topography of the site (slope and foundation)?
- What is the housing availability for workers and managers?
- What environmental factors (schools, cultural, community atmosphere) might affect my business and my employees?
- What will the quality of this site be in 5 years, 10 years, 25 years?
- What is my estimate of this site in relation to my major competitor?
- What other media are available for advertising? How many radio and television stations are there?
- Is the Quantity and quality of available labor concentrated in a given area in the city or town? If so, is commuting a way of living in that city or town?
- Is the city centrally located to my suppliers?
- What are the labor conditions, including such things as relationships with the business community and average wages and salaries paid?
- Is the local business climate healthy, or are business failures especially high in the area?
- What about tax requirements? Is there a city business tax? Income tax? What is the property tax rate? Is there a personal property tax? Are there other special taxes?
- Is the available police and fire protection adequate?
- Is the city or town basically well planned and managed in terms of such items as electric power, sewage, and paved streets and sidewalks?

Page A-8

Choosing the Proper Method of Organization

Listed below are legal forms of business available to the small business entrepreneur:

Sole Proprietorship

Advantages
- Simple to start
- All profits to owner
- Owner in direct control
- Easy entry and exit
- Taxed as individual

Disadvantages
- Unlimited liability
- "Jack-of-all-trades"
- Capital requirement limited
- Limited life
- Employee turn-over

Partnership

Advantages
- Easy to originate
- Credit rating
- Talent combination
- Legal Contract

Disadvantages
- Unlimited liability
- Misunderstandings
- Partner withdrawal
- Regulations

Corporation

Advantages
- Limited liability
- Expansion potential
- Transfer of ownership
- Retain employees

Disadvantages
- Double taxation
- Charter restrictions
- Employee motivation
- Legal regulations

What Is A Corporation?

A corporation is an artificial being, invisible, intangible, and existing only in contemplation of the law," wrote Chief Justice John Marshall. In other words, the corporation exists as a separate entity apart from its owners, the shareholders. It makes contracts; it is liable; it pays taxes. It is a "legal person".

The corporation is the most complex of the three major forms of business ownership. The corporation stands as a separate legal entity in the eyes of the law. The life of the corporation is independent of the owners' lives. Because the owners, called shareholders, are legally separate from the corporation, they can sell their interests in the business without affecting the continuation of the business. When a corporation is founded, it accepts the regulations and restrictions placed on it by the state in which it is incorporated and any other state in which it chooses to do business. Generally, the corporation must report its financial operations to the state's attorney general on an annual basis.

Estimating Start-up Costs

Item	Amount
Fixtures and Equipment	$ ________
Building & Land (If Needed)	________
Store and/or Office Supplies	________
Remodeling and Decorating	________
Deposits on Utilities	________
Insurance	________
Installation of Fixtures	________
Legal Fees	________
Professional Fees	________
Telephone	________
Rental	________
Salaries and Wages	________
Inventory if Retailing	________
Licenses and Permits	________
Advertising and Promotion	________
TOTAL Estimated Start-up Cost	$ ________

Preparing An Income Statement

What is an Income Statement?

The income statement shows the income received and the expenses incurred over a period of time. Income received (sales) comes essentially from the sales of the merchandise or service which your business is formed to sell. Expenses incurred are the expired costs that have been incurred during the same period of time.

Plan A Budgeted Income Statement For One Year

1. Project Total Sales
2. Estimate Total Expenditures
3. Example Listed Below for Income Statement

Percents	1	2	3	4	5	6	7	8	9	10	11	12
Sales												
Cost of Sales												
Gross Profit												
Expenditure												
Rent Expense												
Supplies												
Wages/Salaries												
Utilities												
Insurance												
Depreciation												
Interest												
Miscellaneous												
Net Profit												

Preparing A Balance Sheet

What is a Balance Sheet?

The balance sheet shows the assets, liabilities and owner's net worth in a business as of a given date.

- Assets are the things owned by your business, including both physical things and claims against others.
- Liabilities are the amounts owned to others, the creditors of the firm.
- Net worth or owner's equity is the owner's claim to the assets after liabilities are accounted for.

A Budgeted Balance Sheet For One Year

- List all your business property at their cost to you: these are your assets.
- List all debts, or what your business owes on all your property; these are your liabilities.
- Take your total property balance (Assets), and subtract the total amount you owe (Liabilities).
- The balance is what you own in your business called (Owner's equity).
- Add Total Liabilities (2) & Total Owner's Equity (3).
- Listed on the next page is an example of a balance sheet.

NAME OF BUSINESS
BALANCE SHEET
DATE

ASSETS			
Current Assets			
Cash	________		
Accounts Receivable	________		
Merchandise Inventories	________		
TOTAL CURRENT ASSETS		________	
Fixed Assets			
Land	________		
Building	________		
Equipment	________		
TOTAL FIXED ASSETS		________	
TOTAL ASSETS			1). ________
LIABILITIES			
Current Liabilities			
Accounts Payable	________		
Note Payable	________		
Payroll Taxes Payable	________		
TOTAL CURRENT LIABILITIES		________	
Long-term Liabilities			
Mortgage Payable	________		
Long-term Note	________		
TOTAL LONG-TERM LIABILITIES		________	
TOTAL LIABILITIES			2). ________
OWNER'S EQUITY			
Proprietor's Capital			3). ________
TOTAL LIABILITIES & OWNER'S EQUITY			(2 &3). ________

Page A-14

Marketing The Business

1. Define Your Market
   - Type of Customers
   - Age, Income, Occupation of your customers
   - Type of Trading Area

2. Promotion of Your Business
   - Advertising
   - Setting your Image

3. Customer Policy Plan
   - Develop a Customer Profile
   - Customer Services
   - Customer Needs

4. Pricing Your Products/Services
   - Know all your Costs
   - Know your Profit Margin
   - Know Competitor's Price
   - Know what Return you want on your Investment

5. Sales Promotion
   - Coupons
   - Contests
   - Displays
   - Demonstrations
   - Giveaways
   - Banners

6. Public Relations
   - Newspaper Article
   - Contact Trade Association
   - Radio Promotion
   - TV Promotion

7. Segmentation of your Market
   - Age
   - Occupation
   - Income
   - Location
   - Education
   - Hobbies

Marketing Planning

Outline for Marketing

I. Product/Service Concept:
   a. Name of product or service
   b. Descriptive characteristics of product or service
   c. Unit sales
   d. Analysis of market trends

II. Number of Customers in your Market Area:
   a. Profile of customers
   b. Average customer expenditure
   c. Total market

III. Your Market Potential:
   a. Total market divided by competition
   b. Total market multiplied by percent who will buy your product

IV. Needs of Customers:
   a. Identification
   b. Pleasure
   c. Social approval
   d. Personal interest
   e. Price

V. Direct Marketing Sources:
   a. Trade magazines
   b. Trade associations
   c. Small Business Administration (SBA)
   d. Government Publications
   e. Yellow pages
   f. Marketing directories

VI Customer Profile:
   a. Geographical
   b. Gender
   c. Age range
   d. Income brackets
   e. Occupation
   f. Educational level

Page A-16

Advertising Media

Medium	Market Coverage	Type of Audience
Daily newspaper	Single community or entire metro area: zoned editions sometimes available	General
Weekly newspaper	Single Community	Residents
Telephone Directory	Geographical area or occupational field served by the directory	Active shoppers for goods or services
Direct mail audience	Controlled by the advertiser	Controlled
Radio audience	Definable market area	Selected
Television audience	Definable market area surrounding TV Stations	Various
Outdoor	Entire metro area	General auto drivers
Magazine	Entire metro area or magazine region	Selected audience

Management and Getting the Work Done

1. Define your objective for starting your business.

2. Define your goals: profit growth for first three years.

3. Develop an organization chart of your business.

4. Define your personal needs.
   - Hiring proper employees
   - Training employees
   - Motivation

5. Define all responsibility for each person in your business.

6. Define all authority.
   - Who will hire and fire?
   - Who will select and train all personnel?
   - Who will keep the important records as to inventory, purchasing, sales records, cash records, etc.?

7. Define all laws and regulations that will be requirements for operating your business.

8. Review all duties and tasks with all your employees.

9. Write a summary of all the important tasks that you want to finish in your first year in business.

Sample Organization Chart

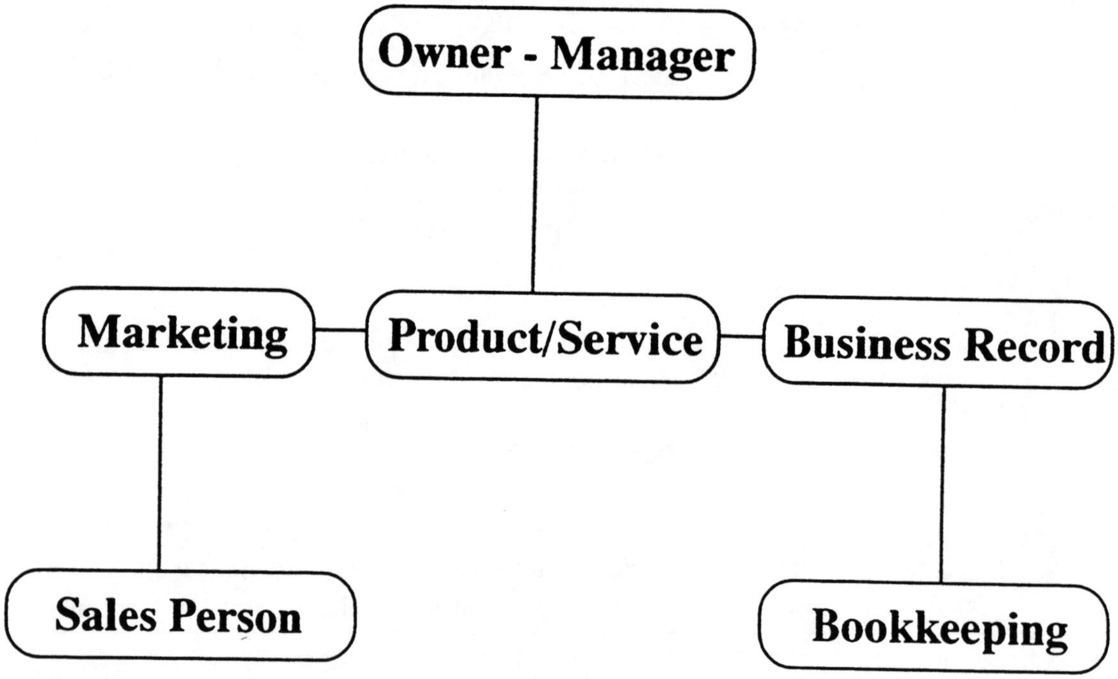

Summary of The Business Plan

Name of Business
BUSINESS PLAN
Date

1. Define your business
   - Name all principals
   - Address and phone number
2. Define your products or services
3. Define your market
4. Define your site or location
5. Advertising Plan
   - Budget
   - Media
6. Chart of Start-up cost
7. Worksheet of Income Statement
   - Revenue/Income
   - Expenses
8. Worksheet of Balance Sheet
   - Assets (Property)
   - Capital (Owner's Equity)
   - Liabilities (Debts)
9. Personnel Outline
   - Number of Employees
   - Staffing & Training
10. Management Organization
    - Organization Chart
    - Evaluation Policy
    - Job Profile
11. Special Statement
    - 3-Year Sales Schedule
    - Cash Flow
    - 3-Year Expense Schedule

Appendix A Summary

1. Contact your State Commerce Department for guidelines in starting your business.

2. Contact your City/County Clerk for guidelines in starting your business.

3. Contact all other Governmental Centers that will furnish you all the legal regulations and tax laws that will effect your business.
   - State Government
   - Internal Revenue Service
   - State Employment Security Commission
   - Department of Treasury
   - City Governmental Units

     a. Fire
     b. Police
     c. Zoning
     d. Building Permits
     e. Health
     f. Water & Sewage

4. Township Government
   - Local Legal Requirements
   - Local Taxes
   - Local Health Permits
   - Local Zoning Laws

Reference Materials

Management Aids Titles

Contact the

Small Business Administration
P.O. Box 15434
Fort Worth, TX 76119

for the following booklets:

- Number 2.025 — Thinking About Going Into Business
- Number 2.010 — Planning and Goal Setting For Business
- Number 1.016 — Sound Cash Management
- Number 1.001 — The A.B.C's. of Borrowing
- Number 1.008 — Break-even Analysis
- Number 2.022 — Business Plan For Service Firms
- Number 2.023 — Business Plans for Retail Firms

Notes

Appendix B

HOUSEHOLD NEEDS

Many small business start-ups fail due to their inability to support their owners. Rarely do new businesses support their owners from the start. However, many individuals fail to recognize this fact. In addition, then, to a sound business plan, it is necessary for an owner to project the household cash needs month-by-month for the first three years of the business' operation. As a new business owner, you should be able to support yourself until your new business is able to support you in a manner to which you are accustomed.

MONTHLY HOUSEHOLD CASH NEEDS

Regular NON-BUSINESS Income

Spouse's salary ________
Investment income ________
Social security ________
Other income ________
Retirement benefits ________
Less taxes ________
Net monthly income ________

Regular Monthly Expenses

Housing
- Mortgage/Rent ________
- Utilities ________
- Homeowner's insurance ________
- Property taxes ________
- Home repairs ________

Living Expenses
- Groceries ________
- Telephone ________
- Tuition ________
- Transportation ________
- Meals ________
- Child care ________
- Medical expenses ________
- Clothing ________
- Personal ________

Insurance Premiums
- Life insurance ________
- Disability insurance ________
- Auto insurance ________
- Medical insurance ________

Debt Repayment
- Auto loans ________
- Consumer debt ________

Discretionary Expenses
- Entertainment ________
- Vacation ________
- Gifts ________
- Retirement contributions ________
- Investment savings ________
- Charitable contributions ________
- Dues, magazines, etc. ________
- Professional fees ________
- Other ________

Total Monthly Expenses ________

Monthly Surplus/Deficit ________

Total Year Surplus/Deficit ________
(Monthly x 12)

Available Assets to Cover Deficit
- Checking accounts ________
- Savings accounts ________
- Money market accounts ________
- Personal credit lines ________
- Marketable securities ________
- Lump-sum retirement/ severance ________
- Other assets ________

Total Assets ________

NEEDED RESERVES

Total Assets-Deficit ________

PERSONAL FINANCIAL STATEMENT

This is a picture of your personal financial condition to date. It is a very important part of any loan application and/or interview, especially when a loan for a projected new business is under consideration.

PERSONAL FINANCIAL STATEMENT

____________________ _____, 19 _____

Assets

Cash	________
Savings accounts	________
Stocks, bonds, other securities	________
Accounts/Notes receivable	________
Life insurance cash value	________
Rebates/Refunds	________
Autos/Other vehicles	________
Real estate	________
Vested pension plan/Retirement accounts	________
Other assets	________
TOTAL ASSETS	$ ________

Liabilities

Accounts payable	________
Contracts payable	________
Notes payable	________
Taxes	________
Real estate loans	________
Other liabilities	________
TOTAL LIABILITIES	$ ________

TOTAL ASSETS $ ________

LESS TOTAL LIABILITIES $ ________

NET WORTH $ ________

BALANCE SHEET

A balance sheet is a current financial statement. It is a dollars and cents description of your business (existing or projected) which lists all of its assets and liabilities.

BALANCE SHEET

______________________ ______, 19 ______

	YEAR 1	YEAR II
Current Assets		
Cash	______	______
Accounts receivable	______	______
Inventory	______	______
Fixed Assets		
Real estate	______	______
Fixtures and equipment	______	______
Vehicles	______	______
Other Assets		
License	______	______
Goodwill	______	______
TOTAL ASSETS	**$**______	**$**______
Current Liabilities		
Notes payable (due within 1 year)	$______	$______
Accounts payable	______	______
Accrued expenses	______	______
Taxes owed	______	______
Long-Term Liabilities		
Notes payable (due after 1 year)	______	______
Other	______	______
TOTAL LIABILITIES	**$**______	**$**______
NETWORTH (ASSETS minus LIABILITIES)	**$**______	**$**______

TOTAL LIABILITIES plus NET WORTH should equal ASSETS

PROFIT AND LOSS STATEMENT

A profit and loss statement is a detailed earnings statement for the previous full year (if you are already in business). Existing businesses are also required to show a profit and loss statement for the current period to the date of the balance sheet.

PROJECTED PROFIT AND LOSS STATEMENT

	Month 1	Month 2	Month 3	Month 4	Month 5	Month 6	Month 7	Month 8	Month 9	Month 10	Month 11	Month 12
Total Net Sales												
Cost of Sales												
GROSS PROFIT												
Controllable Expenses Salaries												
Payroll taxes												
Security												
Advertising												
Automobile												
Dues and subscriptions												
Legal and accounting												
Office supplies												
Telephone												
Utilities												
Miscellaneous												
Total Controllable Expenses												
Fixed Expenses Depreciation												
Insurance												
Rent												
Taxes and licenses												
Loan payments												
Total Fixed Expenses												
TOTAL EXPENSES												
NET PROFIT (LOSS) (before taxes)												

CASH FLOW PROJECTIONS

A cash flow projection is a forcast of the cash (checks or money orders) a business anticipates receiving and disbursing during the course of a month. Well managed, the cash flow should be sufficient to meet the cash requirements for the following month.

CASH FLOW PROJECTIONS

	Start-up or prior to loan	Month 1	Month 2	Month 3	Month 4	Month 5	Month 6	Month 7	Month 8	Month 9	Month 10	Month 11	Month 12	TOTAL
Cash (beginning of month														
Cash on hand														
Cash in bank														
Cash in investments														
Total Cash														
Income (during month) Cash sales														
Credit sales payment														
Investment income														
Loans														
Other cash income														
Total Income														
TOTAL CASH AND INCOME														
Expenses (during month Inventory or new material														
Wages (including owner's)														
Taxes														
Equipment expense														
Overhead														
Selling expense														
Transportation														
Loan repayment														
Other cash expenses														
TOTAL EXPENSES														
CASH FLOW EXCESS (end of month)														
CASH FLOW CUMULATIVE (Monthly)														

Appendix C

Getting Down to Business…

How to Start & Manage a Restaurant Business

An Instructional Guide
for Creating a Small Business
by Jerre G. Lewis, M.A.
and Leslie D. Renn, M.S.

Notes

Table of Contents

Page a

Table of Contents

Page b

Part One

Creating a Restaurant

Page 2

Unit 1: Planning a Restaurant

There are many, many small businesses in America. Small businesses can have as few as one worker (the owner) or as many as four workers. A small business owner is "self-employed." Often a whole family works together in a small business.

There are four things that you will need to do when planning to become a restaurant owner:

- decide what services, customers, and competition the restaurant might have;
- decide what personal qualities and skills you will need;
- know how to compete well; and
- learn about the legal requirements for running the business.

Services, Customers, and Competition

As a restaurant owner, you will be different from most other business owners. You will need to know something about manufacturing, retailing, and the service trades. Most business owners only need to know about one of these areas. Manufacturing will involve a processing job, like preparing the food. After the food is prepared, you will need to sell it to your customers, like the retailer. The food is sold and eaten in the restaurant. So you will have to deal with the problems that occur in the service trades.

Services. A restaurant serves people's eating needs and includes two types of services: "luxury" and "fast food." The luxury restaurant includes family and entertainment types. The family restaurant has good food and service. These things make you relax and feel comfortable. The entertainment type has singers, bands, and "live acts." It usually charges more for meals, too.

The fast food service sells quickly prepared food and deals with a lot of services and customers. These services attract to people who need quick service and tasty dishes at a low price.

Customers. All types of people are likely customers. People want different things from food. Their taste and income are different, so they eat in all types of restaurants. Business workers usually eat in cafeterias where they work. Shoppers and business workers who are in a hurry eat in lunch counters or "fast food" places. Travelers or professional people usually eat in "luxury" restaurants where they can relax. The type of customer you serve will probably depend on your location. The Chamber of Commerce can tell you the number of people in your area and the number of shoppers in a certain area. Just look it up in the Yellow Pages of the telephone book.

Competition. There is a lot of competition in the restaurant business. Competition is one of the most important things to consider in selecting the area for your restaurant. This topic will be discussed in detail later. Visit other restaurants to see what they offer. It will help you decide what "special service" you might need to offer to make your business a success.

Personal Qualities and Skills

Most restaurant owners feel that your personal qualities are the most important part of the business. A lot of owners have succeeded without much education, experience, or management skills. But it is to your advantage to know something about the restaurant business in order to succeed. Restaurants are a people business.

You must:

- really like food and people. He likes preparing food and enjoys being around people. He is courteous, pleasant, and fair to everyone.

- be skilled in buying, preparing, and serving food. He knows where and how to buy good food. He has cooked and served many meals.

- have a head for figures. He knows the cost of food and how to arrive at a fair selling price.

- be willing to work hard and long hours. He has worked two jobs many times.

- have concern for the quality of the food and health of the community you serve. He has always provided the highest standard of service to his customers, no matter how simple the menu.

You may like being with people and working with them. Then you will probably have a good relationship with your customers and employees.

How to Compete Well

New services. Offer new services other restaurant owners do not provide. Here are some ideas:

- special food ideas
- delivery service to nearby businesses only
- the community newspaper
- one free cup of coffee or a multi-vitamin
- a separate area where "kids" can eat.

Special Business Image

Create a business image that people won't forget. Give your restaurant and menu a "catchy" name. Hire friendly employees who care about people and don't mind hard work. Have them remember the regular customers' names. Everyone likes to be remembered. Don't forget a special item for the children.

Legal Requirements

Contact your local Chamber of Commerce to learn the kind of taxes you must pay, the licenses you must get in order to do business, and the regulations you will need to meet. Here is a list of a few of the things you will need to obtain:

- business license;
- health department permit; and
- fire department permit.

You will also want to protect your business and customers by carrying different types of insurance. Talk to a business insurance agent to find out what types of insurance you will need.

Unit 1: Summary

It takes a lot of planning to get a restaurant off to a good start. Now you know some of the things that you must do as a restaurant owner when planning to open your own restaurant.

Unit 2: Choosing a Location

Once you have decided to open your own restaurant, how will you choose your location? Do you have a certain type of restaurant in mind to fit a special location? Or will you try to fit the restaurant to any location?

Things to Think About in Deciding Where to Choose a Location

You should think about the following three things when making your choice:

- competition - the number of other restaurants in the area;
- possible income - how much money can be made; and
- transportation - whether customers will be able to get to the restaurant easily.

Competition

Competition is one of the most important things to watch when you choose your location. Any location may be a bad one if there are a lot of good restaurants. See what kind of menus, special services, prices, and business hours they have before you make a decision about the area.

Possible Income

How much money will you make if you decide to choose a location in this area or that area? You'll need to check the amount of money people pay for rental and home costs for each area of interest. Rental and home costs are usually 20% of a family's income. If a family pays $300 per month, it is probably making about $18,000 a year.

The amount of income spent on food in restaurants varies for different incomes. But the average is about 5%. The family that makes $18,000 a year would probably spend $900 a year in restaurants.

If a neighborhood has 1,500 families making $1,500 a month, a restaurant could make about $100,000 a year. Sounds fantastic, but there may be other restaurants in the area. Then you'll probably have to share the sales with them. Of course, this will depend on how creative you are in making your restaurant a success.

Call or visit the Chamber of Commerce and a real estate office for each of your areas of interest. These organizations can give you information about the income of each community in their area.

Transportation

A restaurant should be easy to get to in order to be successful. To determine this, find out:

- the number of people who pass by on foot or in cars;
- the hours crowds are heaviest;
- where the people are going - home, work shopping;
- the types of businesses nearby;
- plans for growth in the area; and
- public parking spaces.

This information can be gathered by visiting your areas of interest. Talk to everyone - store owners, office employees, shoppers, the person next to you at a competitor's restaurant. You can also contact the city planning department. Talk with someone there about plans for growth in the area and the amount of public parking.

Choosing a Location

In choosing the actual site for your restaurant, there is one thing you will have to do first. Find out if the customers will be able to get to you. If they come by car, parking space is absolutely necessary. Before you decide on the location, "clock the traffic." Count the number of people and cars that pass the spot. Be sure to cover the hours planned for your business. Don't forget about weekends and the effect of weather conditions, good and bad.

In making your decision, it is also necessary to decide on the size of the business you will run and the rent you will pay. The rent should be based on the amount of business (money) you expect to bring in. Your rent should average about five percent of this amount.

If you pay $300 for rent a month, you should expect to take in about $6,000 a month in sales. Your seating capacity, expected turnover, and type of customer may not indicate this sale volume ($6,000). Then choose another location, or change the plans of your business.

The location may meet your requirements. But, before making a final decision, make a map of the area by following the steps below.

- Draw a line around the location to include all other businesses.
- Spot key businesses in the area.
- Make a special mark around eating places so you can tell the size, type, and location of your competition.

Picking a location may be the single most important decision you will make in owning your own restaurant. So plan to put a lot of time into the choice that you make.

Unit 2: Summary

Once you have decided to open your restaurant, you must "check out" the competition, possible income, and transportation for the area in which you plan to set up your business. You will also need to decide on the size of your business and the rent you should pay. Your time and planning will determine the success of your business.

Unit 3: Getting Money to Start

Now that you have located a place for your restaurant, you'll need some money to start it. That is, unless you are very wealthy and don't need to borrow money from anyone. For those of you who fit this case, you may skip this section. But for the "struggling, up and coming restaurant owners of tomorrow," read on.

Let's say you have tried to borrow from friends and relatives, but they just aren't able to help right now. To get the money to start your business, you'll need to go to a lender—a bank or government agency. You will need to provide a lot of information to prove that you are a good business risk. Lenders will want:

- personal background information (a resume);
- a description of your business; and
- a statement of financial need.

Personal Background Information

A resume is the first thing you should prepare when requesting a loan. The resume tells the lender who you are, what you are doing now, and what you've done in the past. The lender needs to know about you to get a better idea of your possible business success.

Business Description

Every new business begins with an idea. Your next step in getting your loan is to put your idea into writing by preparing a written description of your business. Your business description should include the following:

- kind of business and its name;
- services you will provide;
- location of business;

- your competitors (other restaurants in the area);
- who your customers will be;
- your suppliers and how you will pay them; and
- number of employees you will need to hire and your strategy for success.

Statement of Financial Need

Detailed information about starting expenses and the amount of money you have on hand must also be given to the lender.

Starting expenses. The starting expenses will tell the lender the exact amount of money you will need to open your restaurant.

Restaurants' starting expenses vary, depending on the size and type of food offered. Usually profits will be slow in the beginning. It is best to borrow enough money so that you will have an excess on hand. This will help to carry you through the first six months of business.

Unit 3: Summary

When applying for a loan, you will need to provide a description of your personal background (resume), a business description, and a statement of financial need. Your careful planning will be the key to the outcome of your loan request.

Unit 4: Being in Charge

Owning and operating a restaurant business involves many different tasks. The most important is hiring and being in charge of your staff. In this unit you will learn about:

- the general tasks involved in running a small restaurant and the staff you might need;
- sources for finding your staff; and
- selecting the staff.

Tasks

In the restaurant business, you will deal with a lot of different tasks. In the course of one day you may:

- prepare and serve the food;
- arrange for food deliveries;
- place new orders;
- call for repair people;
- hire and train new employees;
- check cash receipts; and
- oversee the kitchen.

Will you be able to handle all these tasks on your own? Being a restaurant owner requires constant supervision of the business. You will need help in handling some of these tasks.

The size of your staff will depend on several things. These include the type of service you offer, your menu, equipment, number of meals served, and the number of customers served each meal. Some restaurants have about one employee to every 50 or 60 customers.

Selecting Job Applicants

The success of your restaurant depends on the skills, cooperation, and loyalty of your employees. You must select from job applicants carefully. Remember, these people will be an extension of you. The success and reputation of your business will depend on how well you make these selections.

Sources of employees. There are several ways to find an employee:

- friends and acquaintances;
- employment agencies;
- newspaper advertisements; and
- personal applications.

Friends and acquaintances are sometimes able to recommend possible applicants. These references are usually the best. They know your business needs and what type of person you have in mind.

Employment agencies are also a good source. There are two types—public and private. The U.S. Employment Service has public employment offices in each state. It is set up for the benefit of both employer and worker. Private agencies usually charge a fee, but some specialize in certain kinds of employment. They might be a good source for getting skilled employees.

The newspaper advertisement is the most widely used way of looking for employees. Another good source would be vocational counselors in schools and vocational programs like home economics and distributive education.

After you have found some potential employees, you will have to learn certain things about them. You can get this information from a detailed application. The applicant should:

- fill out a detailed application;
- provide personal references; and
- have a personal interview.

Detailed application. The amount of detail in the application will depend on the type of job you want to fill. You should look for physical ability, educational background, and personal qualifications.

Physical ability and aptitude for handling tools and equipment are needed in restaurant work. You must look for physical abilities that will help the employees develop the skills they need for the job. Waiters and waitresses, cooks, and busboys and busgirls have to do a lot of walking and standing. So keep in mind that a lot of physical demands will be put on these employees.

Educational qualifications are important. Employees should be able to read and write, add and subtract, and multiply. This is especially true for the employees who will be dealing with the customers and making money transactions. A high school education would be an asset for any staff who may be asked to do a supervisory task.

Personal qualifications involve emotional stability, which is needed for any person who has to work with others. It is especially important in restaurant employees so that you avoid problems when you have periods of heavy and fast work. Energy, conscientiousness, and cooperation are qualities to look for in all of your employees.

Personal Interview

The personal interview is especially important. It can tell you about the personal qualities that don't show up in the application. In your interview you should discuss carefully the job qualifications with the applicant. Through a friendly conversation you can find out how the person meets your standards.

Personal References

Before hiring the person, check his or her references. Remember that hiring a person represents a large investment. An application and interview may show that a person is qualified to do the job. But after you check the references, they may show this is the wrong person to hire.

The best type of reference check is person-to-person. Call the reference and discuss the applicant. Prepare a list of questions to ask. These might include discussing the person's employment record, what kind of employee the person was, and how well he or she got along with others. It takes a lot of time, patience, and skill to check references. But they are the best, most reliable source of information about the applicant.

Employee Training

Employee training is necessary for a successful restaurant operation. No business can succeed unless it is run by a staff of workers who know their jobs and perform them well. Let's suppose that you decide to hire a new waiter without training or experience and he is immediately put to work. He is told to watch the other waiters and do as they do. In a certain period of time the new waiter will learn your system. The amount of time taken to learn this process can be timely and costly to you. The job could have been learned more quickly with the proper training program.

Give the new employee a complete description of the job and a chance to practice before beginning work. The advantage of training is to shorten the learning period and make learning more effective. This contributes to greater production, lowers the cost to you, increases the employee's job security (which means less supervision), and improves his or her attitude about the job.

Unit 4: Summary

There are seven tasks you may do in the course of a day in running a restaurant: preparing and serving the food, arranging for food deliveries, placing new orders, calling for repair persons, hiring and training new employees, checking cash receipts, and overseeing the kitchen. Hiring new employees for a restaurant involves finding new employees, reviewing their applications, interviewing them, and checking their personal references. Training employees contributes to greater production, lowers the cost to you, increases employees' job security, and improves their attitudes about the job.

Unit 5: Buying and Keeping Track of Supplies

One of the most important decisions you will make in owning your own restaurant will be buying food and keeping track of your supplies. Food is the largest part of your business. You will probably spend from 35 to 50 percent of your expenses on it. Food is the only thing you will be selling. So the amount of money you make will depend on how carefully you make your purchases.

You will need to know three things when buying your supplies:

- what to buy;
- where to buy (suppliers); and
- how to buy.

What to buy depends on a lot of things. These include prices, your storage area, and the condition of the food when you buy it. Of course, the only food you will need to buy will be food that is on your menu.

Prices must be considered when making your purchases. If you have to go a long way to buy your food, it can be very expensive. Look for local suppliers. Check out the markets in the area for good buys. Try not to under- or overbuy. Consider the type of "turnover" you might have when buying. The hourly customer turnover rate per seat in a table service restaurant varies between one and two hours.

Quantity is also very important to consider. Buy only the amount of food that can be used and stored properly. Buy by the weight whenever possible. Quality is indicated by grade. The grade indicates the quality at the time of grading. It does not indicate the condition of the supplies at the time of the sale. So you will have to rely on good judgment when making your purchases.

Where should you buy your food? Your food may be purchased from many places. These include:

- wholesale grocers;
- fresh produce suppliers;
- single product distributors; and
- processed food distributors.

These areas will be discussed in the suppliers area of this unit.

How should you buy your food? You can go to the market yourself to see what is available and being sold for a good price. Or you can buy from a salesperson in person or by phone. Good salespeople know the products and are "in touch" with business conditions. They will help to keep you informed about good buys. You may decide to buy by phone. Then set aside a specific time during one or more days of the week for these calls.

When ordering by telephone, be specific. Compare prices or products of the same quality from at least two sources before you place an order. Once you have found a good supplier, set up an understanding. Tell the salesperson to notify you when there is a change in the price list. Try comparing prices with different suppliers and placing orders with different dealers on different days.

Suppliers

You will need to consider three things when you choose your suppliers:

- quality and type of merchandise;
- prices; and
- services provided.

The quality and type of merchandise you buy will depend on your choice of suppliers and distributors. Restaurant owners usually deal with different suppliers. They are wholesale grocers, fresh produce suppliers, single product distributors, and processed food distributors.

Wholesale grocers. These people round up all kinds of nonperishable goods, from sacks of sugar to napkins. They will send a sales representative to your restaurant to discuss the needs of your operation.

Fresh produce suppliers. You can either send an employee with a truck or station wagon to a produce center or arrange for a "service wholesaler" to do the shopping. To place your order, you can call the distributor and reach an agreement on price and delivery date. An order called in on Friday can be set for delivery by the distributor the following Monday. Billing is usually weekly. But this varies with the local market and the distributors.

Single product distributors. These people can be found in the Yellow Pages under the specific product type (milk, poultry, beef, etc.), where there are lists of companies supplying that product.

Processed food distributors. These are listed in the telephone book under "Frozen Foods, Wholesale" (frozen vegetables and entrees), "Food, Dehydrated," or "Food Products."

The Restaurant Association (a trade association) distributes a free buyer's guide listing suppliers. You can contact the nearest trade association officer to find out if additional help is available in locating sources. Restaurant publications are another handy source of suppliers. Also, the "Grocers, Wholesale" ads in the phone book Yellow Pages may give you information about dealers specializing in supplying restaurants.

Supplier Terms

Food suppliers often open charge accounts for good credit risks. Some wholesalers put new accounts on a two-week paying basis until a good record is established. Then they extend credit on a monthly basis. Paying bills promptly, though, is the best way to continue a good relationship with your supplier.

Ordering Food

You should order your food based on a menu pattern covering at least a one-week period. This will allow you to make any recipe adjustments that might come up. For a record of the amounts you will need for a given portion, use a recipe card file. This recipe reference file would list, in alphabetical order, dishes frequently severed, the number of portions, and amount of supplies needed. For example, under "Stew for 50," you would note: 81 lbs. of potatoes, 6 lbs. of carrots, and so on. This file serves to give the cook instruction. It also tells you how much of what to order.

To make up an order for staple foods (sugar, flour, salt), keep a "want" list in a handy spot. Jot down the things you will need. Before placing your order, check to see what food supplies you have on hand. Since fresh foods spoil quickly, they must be used immediately. Make up a "market" list before you telephone or shop. Fill in the prices of the things you buy when you make your purchases.

Inventory Control

Careful recordkeeping can help you work out a system that shows, at any given time, how much food is on hand, how much is on order, and how much needs to be ordered. You will be able to see what supplies are used most frequently and need to be reordered. You will also be able to recognize the supplies that don't sell or are difficult to obtain.

An inventory control system can be based on counting storeroom stock, counting your guest checks, or counting cash register tape sales. You can use the information from delivery invoices to list goods on hand. Shipment dates, cost, and quantities are usually noted on these invoices. Place a check mark beside the name of the items as they are removed from inventory to be used. Inventory counts can be taken daily or weekly, depending on your needs. This decision will depend on your business and what will be easier for you to handle.

If your inventory control system is really working, there will be little food waste. Reducing waste is the result of a balanced inventory plan. Let's say you are ordering the right amounts of goods at the right times. Then you will never need to give your customers dishes made from leftovers—unless, that is, "leftovers" are your specialty.

Unit 5: Summary

Buying food and keeping track of supplies are very important parts of owning your own restaurant business. There are things to know when buying supplies: what to buy, where to buy, and how to buy. Three things must be considered when choosing your suppliers: quality and type of merchandise, prices, and services provided. A purchase order form should be used to record the information you need when ordering your food supplies.

Unit 6: Setting Prices

In setting the prices for your restaurant you will need to think about four things:

- food costs;
- wages and other operating expenses;
- competitors' prices; and
- profit.

In this unit, you will learn about the four main things to consider in setting prices and the way you go about doing it.

Food Costs

In choosing prices for your meals, you need to consider the amount you had to pay for the food and related items you put into the meal. You should make a list of everything you serve in a certain meal and the prices you had to pay for each item. After you figure out the total cost, you usually multiply by three to find out how much to charge the customer.

Wages and Other Operating Expenses

Your prices must allow for your operating expenses. Operating expenses for a restaurant include such things as wages, rent, taxes, insurance, paper and other supplies, advertising, utilities, repairs on equipment, payment on loan debt, and depreciation. Depreciation is the amount that your equipment reduces in value each year due to wear and tear. It applies only to equipment you own.

You will have to pay your employees a minimum hourly wage. Of course, each employee's wages will depend on his or her job and experience. A cook will be paid more than a waiter or dishwasher. The waitresses' and waiters' tips usually make up for their low salaries.

For information on wage requirements contact your state Restaurant Association or the nearest office of your State Division of Industrial Welfare.

Competitors' Prices

Your prices for meals will also depend on what your competition charges. This means restaurants who offer similar meals and services in a similar location. For example, if you charge more for your lunches than your main competition down the block, you'll "price yourself out of business."

Profit

Profit is what is left over after everything else has been paid. In a restaurant with a sales volume of about $100,000 a year, the profit may amount to about $1,500 a month.

Profit includes your own salary, income taxes, and money to expand your business. Out of profit, for example, you would buy new furniture or a new energy-saving dishwasher.

Unit 6: Summary

Setting prices takes some thinking. There are four main things to consider in setting prices: cost of food, operating expenses, competition, and profit.

Unit 7: Advertising and Selling

Advertising and selling your restaurant are very important to the success of your business. As a restaurant owner you will need to do three things:

- initiate the sale;
- understand customer needs; and
- select various forms of advertisement.

Initiate the Sale

Your first step in selling your service once you have opened your restaurant is to meet the customers. Greet them with a friendly smile and give them your immediate, prompt attention.

The actual selling of the food involves introducing the customers to the type of food and services you offer by - you guessed it - giving them the menu. Tell the customers about the food when you answer their questions. Give tactful advice about the food. Never high pressure your customers into selecting a meal they might not enjoy.

Understanding Your Customers

Another important area to think about when selling your services is the customer's viewpoint.

Many restaurant owners work so hard at buying supplies, supervising employees, and serving food that they never stop to look at the restaurant as the customer sees it. They are so busy preparing the meals that they forget how to sell them. They overlook little things that may mean the difference between customer satisfaction and displeasure.

A way to learn what customers think of your food is to look at the plates as they come back from the customers. The food left on a plate will tell you what kind of food people like least. A lot of customers may leave a certain food on their plates. Then you will know something is wrong.

Customers' complaints usually include things like slow service, uncomfortable chairs, rocking tables, bad lighting, and drafts. If customers tell you about their complaints, you can usually correct them. But many won't tell you. They just won't come back. This is the greatest danger a restaurant faces. So invite customers [illegible] suggestions. [illegible] may include an area for suggestions on your menu. Or you might place a box near the door where they can drop their comments.

Advertising

Word-of-mouth is the best means of advertising for the individual owner restaurant. People like to swap stories or recommendations about delicious meals with excellent service. And let's not forget the stories about horrible service and terrible food. Unless you have a full house every day, you will want to do some kind of advertising to attract more customers. Some restaurants don't advertise. But for those that do, 4% of their operating expense is spent on advertising costs.

There are three ways to attract customers to your restaurant: Yellow Pages, newspaper ads, and direct mail.

Yellow Pages. Advertising in the Yellow Pages is absolutely necessary. Your ad will reach the entire community and will last a long time. It should appeal to all types of people.

An ideal ad has several qualities.

- It's simple.
- It's informative.
- It's truthful.
- It shows important or special features of your business.
- It's imaginative and attractive.

These ads get a lot of response from all types of restaurant customers. These include local residents, tourists, people new in town, and those who have lived in the same place for a lifetime. Cost is based on page space.

Look at your competitors' ads. Try to design an ad that will include a headline, information about the restaurant, your name, address, the phone number, and a picture of the place. Remember, the ad order should be placed far enough in advance to appear by the time you open for business.

Newspaper ads. Plan to advertise in the newspaper, at least until your business is well established. Newspaper ads have several advantages.

- They reach a large number of people.
- They are pretty cheap for the number of people they reach.
- They can reach all types of people.

The cost of the ads is usually based on column inches, with the highest for metropolitan dailies and lowest for weeklies. Contact the newspaper display advertising department about detailed information you might need.

Direct mail. This is advertising sent to the customer. Fliers, sample menus, and letters are used in this type of advertising. Direct mail advertising is good because it can be sent to a special group of people who would likely be influenced by it. It is the most personal of all advertising because it is directed to an individual by name.

The advantage of this type of advertising is that the message is addressed and delivered only to people you want to reach at the time you want them to receive it.

Unit 7: Summary

As the owner of a restaurant, you must sell your services to everyone. There are three things you will need to do in selling and advertising your services: initiate the sale, understand the customer's needs or viewpoint, and choose various types of advertisement to use.

Unit 8: Keeping Financial Records

As a restaurant owner, you must have a clear way of keeping track of your income and expenses. You must keep good financial records. Then you will know how your business is doing and you can make better business decisions.

Your records will help you to answer the following kinds of questions:

- How much business did I do?
- How much net profit did I earn?
- How much were my food costs?
- How much were my other expenses?

Many restaurant owners question the need for keeping records. They say, "Why keep a lot of complicated records? I'm so busy running my restaurant, I don't have time for recordkeeping."

Many small restaurants have failed either because of poor recordkeeping or because no records were kept at all. Business success and good recordkeeping go hand in hand. There is a real need for recordkeeping.

Your record system does not have to be complicated. It can be simple, easy to keep, and require little time. You will need to know how to keep track of the money coming in to (cash receipts) and going out of (cash payments) your business. You will learn about guest checks and daily cash sheet.

Guest Check

These checks are sometimes called guest orders. The guest check is the record for the service of your food and the way in which you collect your money from the customers. The check has space for the order and the correct amount to be paid by the customer. It also includes information about the:

- server (waiter or waitress);
- number of guests (customers);
- table being served; and
- date and amount of the purchase.

These checks are usually purchased in "book" form. They should be numbered so that all of them can be accounted for. Guest checks will tell you how many sales you have made in a day. They should also be checked against your cash register receipts at the end of each day. Your cash receipts are your record of each sale plus the total number of checks you ring up.

Daily Cash Sheet

You can use a daily cash sheet to keep track of the money coming into and going out of his restaurant each day. This is a way of recording the cash sales for each day. The sales are recorded on the left side of the form and are added up daily.

On the right side of the form, you enter the money you paid out each day. These are the operating expenses of your restaurant. The actual daily cash sheet that you will use as a restaurant owner may be different.

At the end of each week or month, these daily forms are added up. They are added again at the end of the year to provide a complete statement of your profit and loss.

If you don't want to bother with the recordkeeping part of your business, you can hire a part-time accountant who specializes in restaurant operations. All you need to do is keep a daily record of:

- cash register receipts;
- cash on hand;
- bank deposits;
- cash paid out; and
- checks issued.

Send these records to the accountant each week or month, depending on your set-up. The accountant will prepare the records and financial statements for you.

Unit 8: Summary

Keeping good financial records is a necessary part of running your own restaurant. It involves properly completing a guest check and regularly keeping track of the business income and expenses.

Unit 9: Keeping Your Business Successful

Everyone who goes into business wants to be successful. But how to be successful is always a business owner's problem.

There are three important ways to keep your business successful.

- Make sure you have enough money on hand.
- Keep profit up and costs down.
- Make changes in your business whenever necessary.

In the last unit, you learned how to keep track of cash on a daily basis. Keeping accurate records of your sales and expenses is a "must" in determining profit. The same kind of system can be used on a weekly, monthly, or yearly basis to keep track of your profit. In this unit, you will learn how to keep track of and increase your profit. You also will learn how to change your business to increase your sales.

Keeping Track of Profit

Profit is what you receive for your hard work. It is the amount left over from your revenues (sales) after all of your costs and expenses have been paid. When you add all the figures over the whole year, you will come up with a profit/loss statement.

A profit/loss statement will tell you what your business owes, what it owns, and how much profit you have made over the year. A profit/loss statement will let you know the direction your business is taking from year to year.

The profit/loss statement has five areas:

- <u>revenues</u> - money that comes into your restaurant from retail cash and credit sales;

- cost of goods sold - wholesale cost of the food that is sold to your customers;
- gross profit - amount of money from retail sales after paying the wholesale costs for supplies;
- expenses - money spent in operating the business, including employees' salaries, rent, utilities, advertising, and so on; and
- net profit - amount of money left over from your gross profit after all your restaurant expenses are paid. (Net Profit = Revenues - Costs and Expenses; or Net Profit = Gross Profit - Expenses.)

Changing Your Business to Increase Sales

Changes in customer habits will always have an effect on the restaurant business. Food and energy shortages will be an added problem. So you'll probably need to increase prices from time to time to raise your profits. You might also need to limit your menu or reduce your number of employees. It will all depend on the change you feel will be most effective in increasing your net profits.

You might also want to improve your menu or change your "image." Before trying to make any changes, you'll need to do some research. Ask your customers and your staff what they would think of your ideas for changes. Everybody's opinion helps. Look at the community and your competitors. Study new eating trends.

Sales may be low for many reasons. Thoroughly investigate the reason you feel the need for change. You might make changes in your prices as the economy changes. You might make changes because other restaurants will be raising prices, too. However, you know that you will have to keep up your good service to keep your customers coming.

Unit 9: Summary

You can figure out profits and compare them on a monthly or yearly basis by recording income and expenses on a profit/loss statement. If you want to increase profits you must increase sales, raise prices, or reduce expenses. To increase sales, you may need to improve the quality of or make other changes in your restaurant.

Summary

This module has been about owning a restaurant. People with training in food services can start restaurants. They can run a luxury restaurant or a fast-food restaurant.

To start a small business, you need to do lots of planning. First you have to be sure that owning a small business is right for you. Then you have to decide what services to offer, how to compete, and what legal requirements to meet.

To pick a good location, you have to find out if your customers would come to your restaurant. Then you have to get money to start. That means showing a banker that your idea is a good one.

Being in charge means hiring good workers and training them to perform their jobs well. You should keep track of customer turnover patterns so you can efficiently schedule part-time help.

Setting prices means figuring out the lowest price you can charge and also the highest price. To do this you need information on your expenses and on your competition's prices.

Advertising and selling are the ways you get customers. You can use Yellow Pages ads, newspaper ads, and direct mailings to promote your business image. These are all important ways to help your business succeed.

You should keep good financial records so you will know how the business is doing. Then you can decide if you can expand your business or if you need to cut it back.

Summary

Page 36

To own and operate a successful restaurant, you need training in food services, work experience, and the special business management skills we have covered in this module. If you have not had a course in food management and services, you should take one before deciding to own a restaurant. You can learn business management skills through business classes, experience, or by using the advice and example of an expert.

You may not make a lot of money by owning a restaurant. However, you would have the personal satisfaction of being responsible for your business and making you own decision. Think about how important these things are to you in considering whether you should start your own restaurant.

Appendix D

INSURANCE CHECKLIST

TYPE OF INSURANCE	PURCHASE	DO NOT PURCHASE
PROPERTY INSURANCE:		
Fire	______	______
Windstorm	______	______
Hail	______	______
Smoke	______	______
Explosion	______	______
Vandalism	______	______
Water Damage	______	______
Glass	______	______
LIABILITY INSURANCE	______	______
WORKERS' COMPENSATION	______	______
BUSINESS INTERRUPTION	______	______
DISHONESTY:		
Fidelity	______	______
Robbery	______	______
Burglary	______	______
Comprehensive	______	______
PERSONAL:		
Health	______	______
Life	______	______
Key Personnel	______	______

Special Appendix

Web Site Marketing

Business Web Site
an
Effective Marketing Tool

More than 100 million people use the Internet each day. A website offers help in marketing your small business. Your web site can help level the playing field for small businesses who compete with big businesses. It can enable small business to expand their business nationally or internationally.

What makes a good web site?

A good web site shows by doing; it proves rather than states. Instead of making claims, it provides evidence.

Evidence can take several forms:

- Case Studies showing how your efforts solved a previous client's problems.
- Testimonials from satisfied clients.
- Reprints of articles you've written or reviews of your work.

Education, however, remains the best way to establish credibility. To the extent prospects leave your web site better informed about your product or service, the easier it is to gain their respect (and their purchase order).

Three steps to creating your own business web site.

Today's tools make web publishing accessible to small businesses without programming experience. For example, Microsoft® Publisher 97 includes PageWizard design assistants, web deign elements and design checkers to help your build a workable web site.

Step one:

Choose a structure and a look. Your site should be structured and designed to best tell your story. But where do you start? Using the Page Wizard, you can choose from pre-designed options that can later be customized so that establishing a structure and "look" is easy.

Step two:

Tell your story. Next, simply select the sample headlines and text provided and replace them with words that describe what you have to offer.

Step three:

Check your work and post your site. The design in Publisher 97 goes through your web site element by element, identifying potential problems. Then, the web publishing wizard guides you through the process of posting your web site on the local Internet service provider or on-line service of your choice.

Remember, with millions of web sites, you may have to market your web site as well as your small business to get traffic for your business. The web site can be an inexpensive way of effectively building your small business.

10 tips for Web Site Online Marketing

1. Put up a simple web page.
2. Use a name that will attract people
3. Give away advice and information
4. Have lots of e-mail correspondence
5. Provide customized pages for users.
6. Visit user groups
7. Get on mailing lists
8. Arrange links with related sites
9. Make sure you're in every possible directory
10. Do not "SPAM"

The principals of a Website

In today's business world, a good website is essential to any advertising campaign, but you need to understand, that all websites are not created equal. Nearly any web development company can build you a site that looks good, but if the public cannot locate it, does it really exist?

First off you need to understand that websites are only limited by your imagination, but again I stress, no matter how creative, how interactive, or how great it looks, if the public cannot easily find it, what good is it? Each search engine has created a list of criteria that your site must comply with, in order to be placed in the top 10 listings; this criteria list varies from search engine to search engine and is not made public.

Optimization; The first three rules of any business also applies to websites; location, location, location. 85% of all internet users use the search engines to find what they are looking for.

Nearly 85% of all searches performed in the world go through Google, Yahoo, and MSN, with AOL at a distant 4th with about 8%. This means that the thousands of other search engines share the last 7 to 10%. Less than 3% of the public will search past the 3rd page, therefore it is imperative for your website to work, it must have top rankings!

The 10 second rule; the average internet user will search through 7 sites before finding what they are looking for. Once your site is located, you have approximately 10 seconds to entice the visitor to go deeper into your site. To accomplish this, your home page needs to provide a brief summary of your site. The visitor must be able to scan this page and conclude that your site contains the information they are seeking within that 10 second window. You can always test the success of your home page by checking your web stats and comparing the visitors to pages viewed. If the average is 2 pages per visitor or better, than you know the average visitor likes what they see.

Contact Info; Studies have shown that the average internet user would rather contact you by telephone than by email whenever possible, yet many websites do not contain a phone number or it is buried in the contact us page. A good website will make the contact information available on every page. If your site is intended to be fully automated, then at least display a "take an action" link prominently on each page.

Newsletters; Electronic newsletters are greatly overlooked. A good monthly newsletter will keep your business at the front of their thoughts. Always be sure the newsletter contains a quick link to your website.

As I previously stated, any web company can make a site look good, but only a few websites have the potential to work, to actually tell your story and bring in business.

Although you can buy a website development program, and possibly build your own site, the odds are greatly stacked against you. Less than one thousandth of one percent of the websites out there can be easily located. Another important tip is to hire a company that not only specializes in regional or global optimization (depending upon your market area), but a company that offers an all inclusive annual program with options for future years at a guaranteed renewal price. I have provided the following link to Sutherland's Web Services, (www.sws.tc). SWS, is a good example of an all inclusive, web development firm that specializes in regional optimization. The all inclusive services of Sutherland's includes; hosting, maintenance, updates, design, development, programming and support. Always remember; "If your site cannot be located, does it really exist?

Stephen H. Sutherland
Sutherland's Web Services
www.sws.tc
Steve@sws.tc
231-929-2655

INDEX

Business Books

NEW EDITION 2007

Telephone 1-231-275-7287 • Fax 1-231-275-7242 • lewisjv@centurytel.net
Telephone 1-480-807-9530 • Fax 1-480-830-1187 • lrenn@cox.net

How to Start and Manage:

ISBN 978-1-57916-152-1	An Apparel Store Business
ISBN 978-1-57916-153-8	A Word Processing Service Business
ISBN 978-1-57916-154-5	A Garden Center Business
ISBN 978-1-57916-155-2	A Hair Styling Shop Business
ISBN 978-1-57916-156-9	A Bicycle Shop Business
ISBN 978-1-57916-157-6	A Travel Agency Business
ISBN 978-1-57916-158-3	An Answering Service Business
ISBN 978-1-57916-159-0	A Health Spa Business
ISBN 978-1-57916-160-6	A Restaurant Business
ISBN 978-1-57916-161-3	A Specialty Food Store Business
ISBN 978-1-57916-162-0	A Welding Business
ISBN 978-1-57916-163-7	A Day Care Center Business
ISBN 978-1-57916-164-4	A Flower and Plant Store Business
ISBN 978-1-57916-165-1	A Construction Electrician Business
ISBN 978-1-57916-166-8	A Housecleaning Service Business
ISBN 978-1-57916-167-5	A Nursing Service Business
ISBN 978-1-57916-168-2	A Bookkeeping Service Business
ISBN 978-1-57916-169-9	A Bed and Breakfast Business
ISBN 978-1-57916-170-5	A Secretarial Service Business
ISBN 978-1-57916-171-2	An Energy Specialist Business
ISBN 978-1-57916-172-9	A Guard Service Business
ISBN 978-1-57916-173-6	A Software Design Business
ISBN 978-1-57916-174-3	An Air Conditioning & Heating Business
ISBN 978-1-57916-175-0	A Plumbing Service Business
ISBN 978-1-57916-176-7	A Sewing Service Business
ISBN 978-1-57916-177-4	A Carpentry Service Business
ISBN 978-1-57916-178-1	A Home Attendent Service Business
ISBN 978-1-57916-179-8	A Tree Service Business
ISBN 978-1-57916-180-4	A Dairy Farming Business
ISBN 978-1-57916-181-1	A Farm Equipment Repair Service Business
ISBN 978-1-57916-182-8	A Children's Clothing Store Business
ISBN 978-1-57916-183-5	A Women's Apparel Store
ISBN 978-1-57916-184-2	A Convenience Food Store Business
ISBN 978-1-57916-185-9	A Pest Control Service Business
ISBN 978-1-57916-186-6	A Printing Business
ISBN 978-1-57916-187-3	An Ice Cream Business
ISBN 978-1-57916-188-0	A Mail Order Business
ISBN 978-1-57916-189-7	A Bookstore Business
ISBN 978-1-57916-190-3	A Home Furnishing Business
ISBN 978-1-57916-191-0	A Retail Florist Business
ISBN 978-1-57916-192-7	A Radio-Television Repair Shop Business
ISBN 978-1-57916-193-4	A Dry Cleaning Business
ISBN 978-1-57916-194-1	A Hardware Store Business
ISBN 978-1-57916-195-8	A Marine Retailing Business
ISBN 978-1-57916-196-5	An Office Products Business
ISBN 978-1-57916-197-2	A Pharmacy Business
ISBN 978-1-57916-198-9	A Fish Farming Business
ISBN 978-1-57916-199-6	A Personal Referral Service Business
ISBN 978-1-57916-200-9	A Solar Energy Business
ISBN 978-1-57916-201-6	A Building Service Contracting Business
ISBN 978-1-57916-202-3	A Retail Decorating Products Business
ISBN 978-1-57916-203-0	A Sporting Goods Store Business
ISBN 978-1-57916-204-7	A Retail Grocery Store
ISBN 978-1-57916-205-4	A Cosmetology Business
ISBN 978-1-57916-206-1	A Franchised Business
ISBN 978-1-57916-207-8	An Electronics Industry Consulting Practice Business
ISBN 978-1-57916-208-5	An Independent Consulting Practice Business
ISBN 978-1-57916-209-2	An Independent Trucking Business
ISBN 978-1-57916-210-8	An Accounting Service Business
ISBN 978-1-57916-211-5	A Nursery Business
ISBN 978-1-57916-212-2	A Seminar Promotion Business
ISBN 978-1-57916-231-9	A Bar & Cocktail Lounge Business
ISBN 978-1-57916-214-6	A Wheelchair Transportation Business
ISBN 978-1-57916-215-3	A Fertilizer and Pesticide Business
ISBN 978-1-57916-216-0	A Desktop Publishing Business
ISBN 978-1-57916-217-7	A Crime Prevention Business
ISBN 978-1-57916-218-4	A Gift Shop Business
ISBN 978-1-57916-219-1	A Handcraft Success Business
ISBN 978-1-57916-220-7	A Coin-Operated Laundries Business
ISBN 978-1-57916-221-4	A Property Management Business
ISBN 978-1-57916-222-1	An Auto Supply Store Business
ISBN 978-1-57916-223-8	A Men's Apparel Store Business
ISBN 978-1-57916-224-5	A Temporary Help Service Business
ISBN 978-1-57916-225-2	An Advertising Agency Business
ISBN 978-1-57916-226-9	A Firewood Sales Business
ISBN 978-1-57916-227-6	A Children's Bookstore Business
ISBN 978-1-57916-228-3	A Used Bookstore Business
ISBN 978-1-57916-229-0	A Sandwich Shop Deli Business
ISBN 978-1-57916-230-6	An Instant Print/Copy Shop
ISBN 978-1-57916-231-3	A Gift Specialty Store Business
ISBN 978-1-57916-232-0	A Gift Basket Service Business
ISBN 978-1-57916-233-7	A Hospitality Management Business
ISBN 978-1-57916-234-4	A Hotel Business
ISBN 978-1-57916-235-1	A Catering Service Business
ISBN 978-1-57916-236-8	A Carpet-Cleaning Service Business
ISBN 978-1-57916-237-5	A Window-Washing Service Business
ISBN 978-1-57916-238-2	An Innkeeping Service Business
ISBN 978-1-57916-239-9	An Apartment Preparation Service
ISBN 978-1-57916-240-5	A Kiosks and Cart Business
ISBN 978-1-57916-241-2	A Janitorial Service Business
ISBN 978-1-57916-242-9	A Medical Claims Processing Business
ISBN 978-1-57916-243-6	A Nursing Home Care Business
ISBN 978-1-57916-244-3	A Home Health Care Business
ISBN 978-1-57916-245-0	A Referral Services Business
ISBN 978-1-57916-246-7	A Hair Styling Salon Business
ISBN 978-1-57916-247-4	A Child Care Service Business

Library Discount - 20%
Retail Discount - 20%
$3.00 Postage & Handling
$21.95 Each
www.smallbusbooks.com

How-To Business Books

ISBN 978-1-57916-248-1	How to Buy and Sell A Business
ISBN 978-1-57916-249-8	How to Advertise A Small Business
ISBN 978-1-57916-250-4	How to Write A Successful Business Plan
ISBN 978-1-57916-251-1	How to Finance Your Business for the 21st Century
ISBN 978-1-57916-252-8	How to Market Your Business for the 21st Century
ISBN 978-1-57916-152-1	How to Start & Manage Your Own Business
ISBN 978-1-57916-152-1	How to Start & Manage a Home Based Business
ISBN 978-1-57916-152-1	How to Start a Participative Management Program

To Order Business Plans

Please Remit To:

Lewis & Renn Associates
10315 Harmony Drive
Interlochen, Michigan 49643

ISBN # ____________ Title ____________________

ISBN # ____________ Title ____________________

Name ____________________ Business Book ________

Address ____________________ U.S. Shipping & Postage $ 3.00

City ____________________

State ________ Zip ________ Total ________